the Gathering

David Manuel

ROCK HARBOR PRESS

ORLEANS, MASSACHUSETTS

All photographs in this book
are the copyrighted property of the author
and may not be used without his permission

*To the memory
of a lion in winter,
Bishop Jesse Winley
(1920-1980)*

When we have gone beyond
the fear of death, Christians,
we will be dangerous!

And unto him shall the gathering of the people be.

— Genesis 49:10

Prologue

If any one point in time could be picked at which the direction of Washington For Jesus finally coalesced, it would be the visit that four of its steering committee paid to a certain Senator in January of 1980. He was a new Senator, but no stranger to high public office, and he had a remarkable business record in the private sector as well. Ushering his visitors into his private office, he closed the solid door behind them and listened carefully as they outlined their plan for a rally they were organizing, potentially the largest of its kind ever held.

When they finished, he thought for a moment, then said: "America right now is like a plane going down in flames." He paused to let the words sink in. "I'm not a religious man, but you Christians just may be our parachute. If it opens, we'll be saved; if it doesn't. . ." He looked out the window. "But I'll tell you one thing," he said, turning back, "don't blame the President. Don't blame the politicians. It's *your* fault," he said, pointing to each of them, one at a time. "You Christians, you've had the answer. You've had the majority. Why did you let it happen? If the Church had been to this country what it should have been, we would never be in the shape we are in today."

1

On the Mall

It was an absolutely gorgeous day, that third Friday in April. The temperature on Washington's sun-drenched Mall must have been in the mid-80's — instant summer, two months ahead of time. If only it would hold. . . . Everyone that noontime seemed to be out taking full advantage of it, rediscovering the joy of being out-of-doors, turning a bag lunch into a picnic, strolling or just lazing in the sun on the lush, green grass. There were some who took their lunch breaks more seriously, and these could be seen logging their three, four or five-mile runs. Never had I seen so many joggers in one locale; it was a little like being in the middle of a perpetual road race. But their frowns of perspiring concentration were balanced by the laughter of those engaged in more frivolous pursuits, such as perfecting one's behind-the-back frisbee release.

There was the sound of children, too — a lot of them. This was the time of spring break for a number of school systems, and families had decided to take some vacation early this year, on the chance that Washington's recent spate of good weather would continue. Extending the length of the Mall were two unpaved walkways, just inside its north and south borders, and along these came parents with youngsters in tow, walking west

towards the Washington Monument or east towards the
Capitol, a mile and a half distant. I had seen the Mall several
times before, but never so resplendent or with so many people
enjoying it.

I drove slowly along Jefferson Drive, hoping against hope to
find one of those three-hour parking spaces in front of the
Smithsonian. And then, just as I was about to enter the no-
parking zone in front of the Air and Space Museum, one
appeared. Backing into it quickly and getting out, I slung my
suitcoat over my shoulder and wandered back towards the
Smithsonian. To my right, I heard something that made me
think of a carnival midway — the sound of nickelodeon music.
I looked under the shade trees that lined the Mall, and there, to
my surprise, was a little carousel, going round and round, with
a mother riding next to her fearful little girl, and two other sets
of parents waiting in the shade for their offspring to finish their
ride.

Selecting the base of a tree not far away, I sat down relaxed,
noting the freshness of the warm spring air, and how good
everything smelled. In the distance to my right, the Capitol
shimmered in the sunny haze, more like a vision than a reality.
The same was true of the Washington Monument, in the opposite direction; it seemed to almost disappear against the silvery
sky. I admired its clean, spare lines, as it soared heavenward,
and recalled something my seventh-grade homeroom teacher
had said to us as we had stood not far from where I now sat: the
original design for the Monument had called for it to be
bedecked with columns, domes, and all of the neo-classical
gingerbread that was in vogue a century ago. He had been
tremendously relieved that the present design had prevailed,
and now, squinting up at it, so was I.

I shook my head and smiled. It had been years since I had
recalled that first visit to Washington. But it had made a
profound impact on me, and I found myself remembering the
whole experience now, with a vividness that belied the thirty-

one years which had passed in the interim. About eleven of us — the entire seventh grade of the little boys' school I went to out in Lyndhurst, Ohio — had come to Washington for a week during spring break (which back then was called Easter vacation). I could not remember now exactly what Mr. Hines told us about Washington, but I did remember his almost reverent respect for the shrines of the nation's capital, the well-spring of the greatest democracy on earth — a respect which he considered his sacred trust to impart to each of us.

He succeeded. At the time, the two highlights of the trip were secretly throwing water-bombs out the windows of our rooms in the old Willard Hotel (until we got caught), and watching an FBI agent actually fire a Thompson submachine-gun in the Bureau's underground range. But these were not the things that stuck with us and grew in our national conscience. In subsequent visits, I would frequently be jarred by the recollection that, not only had I been there before, but I was moved as deeply as I had been when I was twelve. The strongest jolt had come just recently, when I had been in Washington for the National Religious Broadcasters' convention. Late one evening, some friends and I paid a visit to the Lincoln Memorial, and as I climbed the white granite steps, I had the eerie sensation of reliving that gray afternoon in 1949, when I had first mounted them. The impact of suddenly coming under the solemn gaze of that huge seated figure had not lessened; it had shocked me when I was a boy, and it moved me now, in ways that I could not articulate. I remembered that Mr. Hines had read aloud the words inscribed on the wall from Lincoln's second inaugural address. I read them again and found my eyes filling, when it spoke of our nation being so torn apart that only God Himself could restore it. "With malice towards none, with charity towards all; with firmness in the right, as God gives us to see the right. . . ." The words had a special meaning in the 1980's, yet in a sense the statue's grieving eyes said it all — then or now.

When our seventh grade returned from that trip, I was the lucky one who got to tell the rest of the school about it in morning chapel. (That was something else we used to do, back then: start the day off with a short service — a hymn, a psalm, a brief talk by one of the older students, some prayers, and a benediction. Chapel seldom lasted more than twenty minutes, but in later years it would become our most cherished memory of the school — just as our headmaster had predicted.) That morning, my talk on Washington was filled with the superlatives of a twelve-year-old who had had a terrific time, but in the intervening years I gradually became aware of how much more Washington really meant to me. I loved Washington. I suspected that it had become as special to me as Jerusalem was to a Jew.

And now I was back again, collecting background material for a book on a rally which would take place on this Mall in just twelve days, a rally which would be attended by several hundred thousand people, most of whom probably felt pretty much the same way about Washington as I did. For their teachers would have come from a similar era and traditions as mine had, and as their teachers' teachers had before them.

I glanced at my watch: one-fifteen. I would have to be going soon. My afternoon would be spent in a hot phone booth with a stack of change, attempting to line up interviews with various Senators and Congressmen, many of whom had never heard of Washington For Jesus. As if by confirmation of that, when I looked over at the area in front of the old Smithsonian castle, I noticed a young couple pointing to the chest-high chain-link fencing that was being put up to provide security for the speakers' enclosure. They asked a question of one of the workmen installing the fence, and he simply shrugged and held his palms up, before turning back to what he was doing. Despite all the efforts of the rally's organization, it remained one of the best-kept secrets in Washington.

To my right, the carousel started up again, and with it that old childhood tune, "The Farmer in the Dell." How did the second verse go? "The farmer takes a wife . . . ." At the time I had learned that song, the farmer and his wife got married with the intention of staying married, till death did them part. Today, the average life-expectancy of one out of two marriages was less than five years — if the young people bothered to get married at all. A lot of them regarded marriage as a big load of unwanted hassles and responsibilities and decided to simply skip it and go right into the pleasures of connubial bliss. In fact, so much had what used to be called "living in sin" become a fashionable lifestyle among the young these days, that if parents professed shock upon discovering that their son or daughter was sharing bed and board, they were invited to leave the stone age and get with the now generation. Some leaders of the women's liberation movement cheerfully predicted the imminent demise of the quaint old custom of marriage, and already in California, more young couples under twenty-five were living together out of wedlock than in it.

I looked up at the pattern the sun was making, as it shone through the leaves overhead. In the larger perspective of all that had happened to the American family, it was difficult to muster alarm at such statistics any more. As a societal unit, the close-knit, caring family of the sort wistfully depicted on TV had once been a reality, the source of America's great strength. Indeed today, the family was still all that was holding the country together, but that common thread appeared to be fast unraveling. It seemed that not just the husbands and wives, but everyone in the home was just putting in time until they could leave. When my parents were young teen-agers, such was God's chain of command that they would not dream of arguing with their parents. But I was a Korean War teen-ager, and times had changed a great deal by then. While we would argue vociferously with our parents at the dinner table, we would nevertheless still be there at dessert.

This was not true of the Vietnam War teen-agers: they

didn't bother to argue; they just got up and left — sometimes for days, sometimes for good. And nowadays, in many families there was no dinner table at all. Instead, it was off to ''fast-food alley,'' or make your own because Mom got held up at the office again. At its best, supper was something on trays together, in front of the TV. For all intents and purposes, in a great many American families, significant communication had ceased to exist. Each individual was now primarily concerned with looking out for number one, struggling to preserve his or her own time and space, even if that meant having to move out.

In short, the American family had ceased to care for its own — at least to the point of giving that concern top priority. An indication of how much we had ceased to care was in the shocking statistics just emerging about the treatment of the elderly. It used to be that a family would keep aging grandparents with them as long as they could possibly care for them within the context of the home. Now they were routinely shipped off to nursing homes as soon as they became a bother. And in many families, where that was not possible, and the tolerance level was especially low, battered elders were beginning to replace battered babies in the headlines. And so, because Americans had forgotten how to care, loneliness at all age levels was becoming a national epidemic. And divorce, now so incredibly easy, did not seem to provide a solution. In my daughter's ninth-grade class, barely a third of the children were still with both their original parents. Many were living with only one parent, who had to work all the harder to support them. Was it so surprising that suicide had now become the second greatest cause of death among young people?

It used to be that society itself exerted a strong supportive influence on the family unit. A town cared for its families; people had a neighborly concern for one another, and it was reassuring to think that help was just a quick shout away. But privacy had now become the goal of all who could afford it —

enough land in the suburbs so that one did not have to see one's neighbor, or a penthouse in the city, so that no one else shared your elevator on your floor. The irony was, of course, that once a man had secured his seclusion (and you could actually do this anywhere by simply "deading out" those who lived nearby), to share with just his family, all too often his children couldn't bear the thought of having to spend another evening with him and would find an excuse to be elsewhere. Which would leave him and his wife (if she, too, wasn't busy doing something else) spending mindless hours in front of the tube. Marathon TV-watching often became the norm for the family which had everything. Familial loneliness may not have been as true in strong Christian households, yet a rapidly increasing number of children from church-going families were being evangelized by the world.

A breeze rustled through the leaves overhead, and a cloud briefly hid the sun. The temperature seemed to drop several degrees instantly, and I shivered at this abrupt reminder that it was April, not June. On the breeze came the sound of the carousel and I recalled the next verse of that childhood song: "The wife takes a child. . . ." So today's kids left home as soon as they could and groped their way into what they hoped would be "meaningful relationships." And if a baby started to come, they simply got rid of it. It was the easiest thing in the world to do now; just go down to the nearest abortion clinic, tell them your sad tale, and. . . the wife takes a life.

Back when I was in high school, abortion was a word you hardly even heard whispered; it was generally regarded as an act akin to premeditated murder. But today abortion was supposed to be a guiltless option, available to any woman on demand. And if she couldn't afford it, legislation was being proposed that would make the government pay for it. *Nothing* was to interfere with her right to do whatever she wanted with her body and what was in it. Indeed, Planned Parenthood affiliates who were administering sex-education curriculums in public schools were emphasizing that teen-agers did not need parental consent to obtain abortions. Yet to suggest that one sure way to avoid the need for abortion was to avoid fornication, was to invite a storm of invective for daring to imply that a woman might curb her "freedom of sexual expression." And so, this year a million and a half lives would be snuffed out, and if the bill for federal funding of abortions passed, every taxpayer in America would become an accomplice.

Angry now, I got up and started walking towards the Monument. *What had happened to us?* Our morality, or what was left of it, was only one measure of our precipitous decline. You could confine yourself to just what had happened to us militarily in the past eighteen years, as we, through idealistic wishful thinking, deluded ourselves into believing that the Russians were as interested in achieving world peace as we were (or could at least be persuaded into becoming so). You could look at our international diplomatic stature: once the hope of every downtrodden nation — the champion of the free world, no less — now, in hardly any time at all, we had become despised by the very nations that we had tried to help, and an embarrassment and increasingly dangerous risk to our allies. Economically, our currency had once been the standard by which all others were measured. Now our economy was behaving like a roller coaster with loose wheels, and our economists were powerless to predict with any accuracy what it was going to do next, let alone bring it under control. As for violent crime, there was a time when it was safe to go out at night, and many Americans even left their homes and cars unlocked. Nowadays, those homes were becoming armed camps, with the sales of security systems and guard dogs never higher.

One could go on indefinitely, but still the most telling indicator was our morality, for the moral state of a nation was a window to its heart. What had happened to America's morality in one generation was simply beyond belief. Twenty years ago, one of my wife's classmates was expelled from college for smoking in her room. Today, a girl in that same women's college could entertain a male guest in her room all night, if she chose to. Such had become our promiscuity that venereal disease had reached the epidemic level. Ten million cases were reported last year, and heaven only knew how many more went unreported. Gonorrhea viruses were mutating into strains that were impervious to the most advanced antibiotics, and now herpes disease, for which there was no known cure, was becoming the new sexual leprosy. Again, there was one sure safeguard: follow God's guidelines and confine sex to the marriage bed, but. . .

Pornography was keeping pace with the times. A PG-rated movie which was acclaimed best picture of the year contained a self-abuse sequence which would have had its distributors thrown in jail a generation ago. Ironically, that left the hardcore purveyors having to roll up their sleeves to reach ever deeper into the cesspool. They had, of course, proven themselves equal to the challenge. Boasted the producer of a multimillion-dollar epic, starring well-known actors, that played in our town recently: "Next to it, your conventional X-rated movie is like comparing 'The Gunfight at the OK Corral' to World War II!" Most sickening of all was the rise of child porn, and yet this, too, was but a mirror of what was happening in our society: the sharpest increase in pregnancies was at the eleven-year-old level.

I had reached the base of the Monument, and stood in its shadow, gazing back at the Capitol, so beautiful in the hazy distance. *Why had it all happened? How could it have happened so suddenly, almost without our noticing?* As if in answer to the latter, the shadow of a cloud passed slowly down the Mall. It took a couple of minutes to travel that mile and a half, and as I watched it, I was reminded of a study in time-lapse photography I'd seen once, years before. A movie camera had been rigged to take pictures of the sky at the rate of one frame per second. When this film was later projected at its normal rate of 34 frames per second, the clouds raced across the heavens, bounding and rolling like a huge surf, breaking on the shore. I had been stunned and had to remind myself that those violently interacting formations were indeed clouds.

What had happened in America was that the indicators of our national disintegration had been observed gradually, on a day-by-day basis over the span of a generation, one frame at a time, as it were. In order to see what had happened to us in historical perspective (or in God's, where a thousand years was as a day), we needed to re-run the film at 34 frames per second. Imagining that, it seemed to me that no major civilization in history had ever deteriorated so quickly!

Why — more than ever now, I wondered why. As I headed back towards where I'd left the car, I reflected that the American Dream had reached its highwater mark in 1963, with the Presidency of John F. Kennedy, but the internal decay had actually begun a long time before. The husk of the seed was still intact, but the spiritual vitality at the core of this nation had withered. We were living in accordance with a code of conduct to which Americans had subscribed for generations without questioning it, but it was just that: a code, an empty husk, devoid of life. The deep wellspring of selfless, renewing Christian commitment which had once been the norm for so many of our ancestors, had for the most part dried up.

To be sure, the majority of Americans still believed in God, and when asked by Mr. Gallup, 53% would admit to having had a "born-again" experience. But how many of us lived each day of our lives as if the Lord were returning tomorrow? How many of us prayed about our decisions, small as well as large, and when His will conflicted with ours, invariably chose His? How many of our lives were surrendered to Him unconditionally? There was a time when the majority of Americans did live that way, or at least tried to. In our book, *The Light and the Glory,* Peter Marshall and I had documented this through countless thousand first-hand sources — diaries, letters, sermons, journals and books. The people who first came to these shores did so out of obedience to a direct leading from God. They came in response to His call to form a Christian nation that would be a light on a hill to the rest of the world. They had faltered, they had fallen back, but they had persevered, and the United States of America was born as one nation under God.

For many generations Americans continued to put Christ first in their lives. They, too, had their times of backsliding, but God was always able to get their attention, through a drought, or a plague of insects, or a war, or some other shared catastrophe. There would be soul-searching and repentance, followed by revival, and the revivals that swept this land brought literally millions back to the foot of the Cross. But then, after World War I ("the war to end all wars," which would "make the world safe for Democracy"), as God poured out His blessings upon His obedient children, with whom He was well pleased, we entered into a period of unparalleled and unprecedented prosperity. And proceeded to get drunk on it. As one of the great Puritan preachers had once put it: "Piety gave birth to prosperity, and the daughter devoured the mother."

We became proud and supremely self-confident. Technology was the new watchword, and the symbol of the age was the high-tension pylon — endless files of them, traversing mountains and prairies, carrying power from unseen hydroelectric dams to unseen metropolises. They began to appear in the giant, metaphysical murals that adorned the walls of civic buildings of that era, along with other fruits of the new technology — flying boats and oil derricks and radio beacons and streamliners. And it all sprang from the cleverness of man's mind, which seemed just about infinite. The scientists were promising solutions to all our problems, and we believed them and turned to them, where once we had turned to God.

But somehow it seemed that for every problem they solved, they seemed to create ten more that no one had been able to foresee, and when, at last, they were confronted with this, they said, in effect, "Well, we're not God, are we?" No, they weren't. But for too long we had regarded them as if they were.

God had tried to get our attention. The Great Depression was a chastisement that should have turned us back to Him, repenting for our greed and lasciviousness and our haughty opinion of our resourcefulness and intellect. But for the first time in our history a calamity of this magnitude was not sufficient to touch all of our hearts. The top echelons of our society had accumulated so much that, while they were straitened, they were not bowed or humbled, let alone brought to their knees. It was to this sector of society that we traditionally looked for leadership, but if our leaders saw no reason to call us to repentance. . . . And after we emerged from World War II as the most powerful nation on earth, we were more confident in our own abilities than ever!

Yet it was not just pride and self-confidence, technology and greed — those things alone could not have separated us so far from the God whom we once trusted so implicitly that we proclaimed it on our currency. There was another element at work here, one that had taken root in the Twenties and had grown quietly and steadily ever since, until it held sway over much of the institutional thinking in America. Some called it liberalism, but many who were a party to it were conservative by nature. Others referred to it as humanism, which was closer, but a great many believing Christians were also a party to it.

To me, it seemed that the most apt description of it was *idealism* — a culmination of wishful thinking that began with the underlying belief that man was basically good. Give man a chance to exercise the latent goodness that was there, and. . . . From this hypothesis, all else proceeded, including the doctrine of *fairness*, which, followed to its end, proposed to legislate behavior which, in a truly Christian society, was spontaneous and inspired. God was not a factor in the idealist's equation, because God was demonstrably unfair in so many of His dealings with men and nations. But once you accepted the innate goodness of man, the Brotherhood of Man *was* possible without the Fatherhood of God. Or so the idealist fervently wished to believe. And so strong was his faith that over the past forty years he had gained influence over the majority of his countrymen, including a great many Christians.

Opposing the idealist stood the Christian realist, who accepted what the Bible said as the literal truth: that man was a fallen creature. Man had a basic, sinful nature, and though he could be redeemed by the Saviour and cleansed and forgiven, that nature was still there. Like Paul, he continued to do the things that he knew he ought not to do, and not do the things that he knew he should do. Indeed, there was no good thing in him, save Christ, and Him crucified. The Christian who really knew that about himself — that given the circumstances, he was capable even of murder — also knew how much he needed Christ daily, and what a blessing confession and repentance could be.

But a lot of Christians had forgotten this. They had come round to the idealist's way of looking at things: that man, especially Christian man, really *was* good, once he had been saved. Blinded by wishful thinking where his own nature was concerned, the Christian idealist thus found it very hard to be wrong (i.e. a sinner), and was therefore privately uncomfortable at the prospect of a need for personal repentance. And since he was confident that doctrinally he was basically right, it stood to reason that any other Christian who did not agree with him was basically wrong. Was it any wonder that there was so much bitter division in the Body of Christ?

As a result of not wanting to look at its own sins, individually and corporately, the Church in America had grown so ineffectual that they could no longer function as a check or balance to the idealists who were now beginning to impose their own version of morality on the rest of us. Indeed, the Church was reminiscent of a shorn Samson rushing forth to do battle with the Philistines and not realizing that his strength had departed.

I had wondered how it happened, and now I had the answer. God was calling us to repent, which meant to turn and go in the opposite direction, in the spirit of II Chronicles 7:14. And He had been waiting a long, long time for us to hear Him.

If my people, who are called by my name, will humble themselves and pray and seek my face, and turn from their wicked ways, then I will hear from Heaven and will forgive their sin and heal their land.

"His people," called by "His name" — that meant us, not the idealists. They had been faithful to the dictates of their faith; it was we who had not been. There had been so much jealousy and back-biting and judgment and mistrust and gossip among Christians — and such a strong desire to persist in these wicked ways — that I really wondered if we could ever do anything together, let alone unite in repentance.

Well, I thought, as I unlocked the car, we would know on the 29th. Behind me, I could still hear the wheezing strains of the carousel. . . .

2

Getting Involved

I spent the rest of that Friday afternoon, the 18th of April, in a phone booth, calling the offices of various Senators and Congressmen. Initially, I was surprised at how accessible they appeared to be, or at least how gracious their phone receptionists were. But gradually, as I was shunted from one assistant to another, I came to see that their accessibility was largely illusory — which only made sense: these men probably had more demands on their time, from more unexpected directions, than any other group in the country. For all that, as I swept the remaining dimes into my hand and creakily stood up, I was suddenly grateful that I was not called to be a Washington lobbyist. After two and a half hours of phoning, I did not have one firm interview lined up.

I was staying with old friends in Alexandria, Virginia, and judging from the Friday afternoon rush-hour traffic, it would be a good hour before I got there. No matter, the car had air conditioning, and there was no urgency. I settled into the traffic that was edging its way over the bridge and relaxed. It was one extraordinary string of coincidences that had brought me here, I thought idly, and how quickly it had all fallen into place. My mind went back to that Sunday evening in February, ten short weeks earlier. . . .

Dean was piloting the ancient Cadillac expertly over the icy roads, as we drove through the crisp, clear night. In the back seat was an old friend from Arizona, John French, and we were busy bringing each other up to date, as Christian friends do when they haven't seen each other for months. Dean and I were partners in a small but growing Christian publishing company called Rock Harbor Press. We had published only four books in the three years since we started, but happily two of those had been bestsellers — *3D* by Carol Showalter and *Hell Bound* by Don Wilkerson. On this trip we were on our way from Cape Cod to New York and then New Jersey on business, and John had agreed to come with us. A successful business-man based in Phoenix, he had an unusual gift for helping Christian businesses get launched on a solid footing, and he had done much organizationally to make sure that we stayed in the black.

Three hours had passed in animated conversation, and now there was a lull as we crossed the Thames river on I-95. Out-side, the night was well below freezing, and I was grateful for the warmth and coziness of the old leather seats. As we approached Branford, I happened to mention something I had seen a month earlier at the National Religious Broadcasters convention in Washington, D.C. It was a booth called "Washington For Jesus," and, curious, I had stopped to chat with the two bright-eyed, cheerful young ladies who were man-ning it. I learned that there was going to be a rally on the Mall in Washington at the end of April, and that it would be the biggest of its kind ever held.

They had handed me a packet of literature which I glanced at skeptically; it seemed to confirm my initial impression which was that the whole thing was a bit kooky — probably someone trying to capitalize on the recent annual Jesus celebrations. If so, they would discover that that idea was past its prime. And who was this John Gimenez who had come up with the idea, anyway? I'd never heard of him. I was about to slip the material into my briefcase (I would throw it away later, when I got back to my room; no point hurting their feelings), when my eye fell on the steering committee. Pat Robertson, Demos Shakarian, Jim Bakker, Jack Hayford — whoever John Gimenez was, he had managed to line up some pretty heavy support. Well, maybe it could be something, after all. They had said that they were "believing for" a million Christians to come. Well, even if they got only a hundred thousand, it might still be fun to go to. Maybe there would be enough in it to do an article. . . .

I had forgotten to throw the information packet away when I got home, but I had put it out of mind, until that night. "Say, John, have you ever heard of something called 'Washington For Jesus'? It's a rally they're having in Washington, April 29th, and I was thinking that maybe I'd see if I could cover it for one of the magazines —"

"An *article,*" he cut me off. "You ought to be thinking about doing a book!"

"Huh?" I wondered if I'd heard my cautious, conservative friend in the back seat correctly. "Come on, John, you can't be ser—"

"I am serious! Washington For Jesus is going to be an historic occasion. Even more so than the Kansas City Conference that you two did the book on in '77."

"How come you know so much about it?"

"I'm the administrative assistant to Arizona's state coordinator for Washington For Jesus, who also happens to be my pastor."

"You're kidding! You're involved?"

"You bet I am! In fact, that's what I'm spending most of my time on right now. Arizona was a little late getting started, and my pastor and I inherited this assignment just a month ago. But it looks like we're going to have two busloads signed up before too long."

And now Dean, who had remained silent thus far, concentrating on the road, spoke: "John, do you really think there's a book in it?"

"Yes, I do. I don't know whether they're going to get the million people that they're hoping for; no one knows. But even if they get only a couple of hundred thousand, that will still be larger than any rally that's ever been held on the Mall, or anywhere else in the country, for that matter."

"Bigger than that anti-Vietnam rally in the Sixties?" I asked incredulously.

"That one, and the Pope's visit, were both just under two hundred thousand."

Dean glanced up in the rear-view mirror at John's silhouette. "Is God really in this, John? It sounds pretty wild."

"I'm convinced of it," came the reply from the back seat. "One prayer group, praying about Washington For Jesus, received a strong word of prophecy, concerning David gathering the five smooth stones and his taking aim, not at Goliath's chest or stomach, but squarely at his head. I can't remember the exact words, but the gist of it was that if anything was to be accomplished, that was where we needed to take our concern, to the head of this nation — to Washington." He paused. "I wasn't there myself, but it did witness to me, when I heard about it."

That seemed to satisfy Dean for the moment, but I was still skeptical, and tried another tack: "How's it being organized?"

"Mostly through the Rock Church," John replied, and I recalled that that was the church that John Gimenez was pastor of in Virginia Beach. "They have a liaison person assigned to work with each state coordinator, also a youth coordinator, and a spiritual coordinator."

"A spiritual coordinator?"

"Yes, they're trying to get a thousand Christians in each Congressional district to pledge themselves to uplift their Congressman in prayer, every day. They plan to get these people to sign a list of intercessors, and delegations will then present them to each Congressman the day before the rally."

I whistled. "That's beginning to sound an awful lot like a Christian lobbying effort."

"Well, it may have started out that way," John admitted, "but honestly, all they're going to do is just give them the list of names, and ask if they might say a prayer with them."

I remained unconvinced. "You know as well as I do, that even if politics are never mentioned, they're going to get the message. Politicians are politicians; they size up potential voters instinctively. And if what you say is true, they're going to be sizing up an awful lot of them who have spent a lot of time and money to come to Washington. And those are people who will care enough to go to the polls on election day." I looked out the window, as the lights of New Haven appeared up ahead. "But I still don't see why you think it's going to be so historic."

Before John could answer, Dean reminded us how late it was, and we focused our attention on finding the right exit for our favorite steak house. It wasn't until we had found it, gotten a table and started on our salad, that I could return to my last question: "I still want to know what's going to be so historic about it."

John ground some pepper on his salad, and cleared his throat, as was his custom before saying something important. "Two things: first, as of last week, it looks like the evangelicals, led by Bill Bright, are coming on board. Men like James Robison of Dallas, and Adrian Rogers, the head of the Southern Baptist Convention —"

"Now *that* is historic!" I exclaimed. Never in my recollection had evangelicals joined forces with charismatics for a common goal, although I'd occasionally seen it happen the other way around, with local charismatics joining evangelicals to help organize for a Billy Graham crusade. But to think that Bill Bright, the head of Campus Crusade . . . .

"Secondly," said John, smiling now, "while Arizona may have been one of the last states to get its act together, if the enthusiasm back home is any indication of what's going on in the other states, what you're seeing is more than the making of a rally. It's a groundswell movement of awakening Christians, the likes of which this nation has never seen!''

Dean put his fork down with a clatter. "Now that's exciting! Because I think I can see what you're talking about. I grew up in a little town called Shelbyville, in Illinois, where my father ran a grocery store. And I can imagine a man like me, being —say— a farmer out in Iowa, who cares about the Lord, and about what's happening to America, but feels powerless to do anything about it, being so far away from the center of things. I mean, what can he do? He's just one man. But then along comes a chance like this, a chance for folks just like himself to come to Washington, and gather together in prayer. It's a chance, maybe the only one he'll ever get, to personally do something for his country, to stand and be counted — for Christ,'' and his voice broke.

I couldn't help but be moved by what Dean was saying. From helping his father in the store, he had gone on to become a division president of a large corporation, before putting all that behind him and moving to the Cape. Yet throughout, he had retained his homespun simplicity, like a modern-day Will Rogers. When he described that farmer from Iowa, he really knew him.

"Now," John said briskly, "the first thing we need is a time-table. How soon could we have finished books?''

"Wait a minute," I said, getting annoyed, "what's this 'we'? *I'm* the one that would have to do the writing, and I've got two other people's books which I have to finish editing, in time to get them ready for our Christian Booksellers Convention in July. May, June and July are the worst possible months for me to start writing anything.''

But John went on as if he hadn't heard a word I'd said. Turning to Dean, he chuckled. "You're just going to have to lock him in a little room in the basement, and give him one meal a day — which he doesn't get until he shoves a chapter under the door."

"Very funny," I muttered, as Dean and John laughed uproariously. I finished my steak in silence.

Eventually, when we were back on I-95 and heading into New York State, I was finally able to enter into their enthusiasm for the project, albeit to a lesser degree, and eventually the conversation shifted to other things, and I was able to forget about Washington For Jesus — until breakfast, a couple of mornings later. It dawned a dazzling day, very cold, but very clear. We had wrapped up our business in New York successfully, and to celebrate, it was decided that, instead of skipping breakfast or just grabbing some toast and juice along the way, we would have an elegant breakfast in the Edwardian Room of the Plaza Hotel, before departing for New Jersey.

The air outside was bracing and invigorating, and New York never looked better, as we walked along Central Park South towards the Plaza. There were bits of mica in the concrete of the sidewalks of New York, and on certain bright days these bits seemed to sparkle like diamonds. This was one of those days. We entered the tall-ceilinged dining room, and there amidst snowy white table linen, cut-glass water goblets, and understated decor, we ordered a breakfast fit for three kings — or oil sheiks. We had fresh strawberries with double cream, and fresh-squeezed orange juice. We had eggs benedict, and light, flaky croissants with sweet butter and four kinds of jam, and the best-tasting coffee in New York. And everything was done perfectly. The waiters, though numerous, were unobtrusive; indeed, the entire dining room was filled with well-dressed people who looked like they never had to be anywhere in a particular hurry.

I was about to comment that this was the best breakfast that — when John, who held onto unfinished business with the tenacity of a pit bull terrier, spoiled it all by getting back on the subject of the Washington For Jesus book, specifically on how much research would have to be done beforehand. What were my thoughts on that?

"Well, to be honest, I haven't given it any thought," I sighed, putting down the croissant to which I was about to apply some tangy-looking, rough-cut English marmalade. "But *if* we get the green light from the Washington For Jesus people — and frankly to me that seems a much bigger 'if' than it does to either of you two — then I would see going down to Virginia Beach as soon as possible and spending a few days there, being with John Gimenez and picking up detailed background. But don't forget, I'll be going down to Bermuda for five weeks, to write that novel I told you about." I slid quickly over that part and continued. "I'll get back around the middle of April, at which time I suppose I would go to Washington, to get the build-up of expectation there. Two weeks should be plenty of time for . . . ." My voice trailed off, as I noticed John slowly shaking his head.

"I think," he said in measured, matter-of-fact, tones, and clearing his throat again, "that you had better forget about going down to Bermuda. You won't be writing the novel then, either there or anywhere else."

My knuckles whitened around the butter knife. "Then *I* think you had better forget about my writing that book!" I tried to keep my voice as modulated and controlled as his, but did not succeed. "I have had to put that novel off twice, and I am not about to postpone it again!" I became aware that silence had spread like ripples to the surrounding tables, and seated at its vortex, I could almost hear the echo of my last words. All around us, people were discreetly turning in our direction, endeavoring not to give the appearance of staring. I felt like I was in the middle of an E.F. Hutton commercial.

I said no more, but ate the rest of my breakfast and struggled to regain my composure. It wasn't easy; they could not begin to understand how much that novel meant to me. All my life, I realized, I had been waiting to write that novel. In the seven years since I had given up the editorship of Logos in order to write, I had written nine books, including a bestseller, but most of them had been with other people. Even the ones I was the sole author of had been dictated by the subject material. But the novel — it would be 100% creative, my first and perhaps only chance to do something that was entirely my own — and God's, of course. I was convinced that He had not merely granted me permission to write it, but had called me to do so, and that His Spirit had guided and inspired the plotting of it. The detailed outline was already completed; all that remained to be done was the actual writing. And it couldn't be more timely, for its intent was to dramatize, in contemporary terms, for secular as well as Christian readers, just how close America was to self-destruction.

The people at the tables nearby had resumed their desultory conversations, but at ours the silence had grown heavy. Well, let it, I thought; I was not going to abandon this novel. Fiction — novels, short stories, plays, television dramas — was the most persuasive tool in the writer's kit, provided he knew how to use it. Sartre and Camus had taught me that. They had each resorted to fiction to get their existentialism across to the broadest possible audience, because they knew that any point made viscerally, going in through the heart, was going to pene-trate deeper and last longer than any point made through the intellect, no matter how eloquently phrased. Harriet Beecher Stowe might have made a thousand speeches against slavery all across the northern states and not had one-thousandth the impact of her novel *Uncle Tom's Cabin*.

I glanced at John and Dean, who were staring fixedly at their plates, finishing in silence, apparently waiting for me to make some sort of apology, or at least modify my outburst, which I was not about to do. Finally, John set his knife and fork neatly on his plate, folded his napkin along its original creases, and said, "With the spirit of adamacy that's present at this table, there's no point in any further discussion of a book on the Washington For Jesus rally."

Good, I thought. I resisted the urge to point out that there was no such word as "adamacy."

And then Dean, who had not yet gotten into it, looked me in the eye and said, "You'd better ask yourself who you're really writing that novel for. Because it sure doesn't sound like you're doing it for the Lord. Maybe you'd better pray about it."

That was all he said, but it was enough. I knew — and I knew that he knew — that if I suspended my anger long enough to pray, there was a good chance that God Himself might tell me to put the novel aside — again — and that He had something else He wanted me to be doing now.

But I did not feel like hearing that from God or anyone else, just then. Instead, I chose to remain angry and carried on with my silent temper tantrum. Dean and John simply ignored me. All the way to New Jersey, they laughed and joked in the front seat, while I glowered at the backs of their heads. And the more miserable I felt, the happier they seemed to get. Finally, just before we got out of the car for our business appointment, Dean turned to me and said, "Don't you think it's about time you came out of your snit and stopped behaving like a spoiled brat?"

At that moment, though we had been close friends and partners for seven years, I would gladly have slugged him. But back home on the Cape, we belonged to a small Christian community, where the members had covenanted to live in the light with one another, no matter what the cost. That meant speaking the truth in love, even if sometimes, like now, that meant tough love. It was painful at times, but it made for incredibly durable relationships. At the moment he spoke, I resented Dean mightily for what he'd said, and the way that he'd said it. But deep down, I knew he was right. And I knew that I would again love him in Christ for having cared enough for me to risk my enmity and say it as strongly as it needed to be said, to get through to me.

Besides, I had been angry and wrong enough times before in my tour in Christ's army, as it were, to know that very shortly I would be back where I was supposed to be, in His formation, marching to His cadence. Happily, the time had long since passed when I would wish that I had never signed on and wonder how one mustered out. No, I had joined up for life, and it was time to get on with soldiering. I didn't always like my marching orders, but then, who did? But it usually didn't take long to adjust to a new assignment, and before long, it would seem like the best duty one could possibly ask for.

I nodded to Dean, and inwardly commenced to work things out with God. By the time we went inside, I was able to look at them and say, "Hey, you guys, I'm sorry." And I meant it.

3

The Green Light

Somehow, I had gotten the rather haughty idea that once *I* had finally agreed to set my plans aside and do a book on the rally, all the other pieces would simply fall into place. This did not prove to be the case. Funny thing — just as we had never heard of John Gimenez and the Rock Church, so they had never heard of a little publishing company on Cape Cod, called Rock Harbor Press. Not overly impressed with our proposal, John Gimenez referred us to the director of communications for Washington For Jesus, John Gilman.

This John proved exceedingly difficult to get hold of — our letters went unanswered and phone calls were not returned, until we finally began to wonder if God wasn't trying to tell us something. Heretofore, whenever I'd been about to embark on a book project that I wasn't certain was in the center of God's perfect will for me, or if I felt that the first draft was getting away from the course and direction it was supposed to be taking, I would pray for open door/shut door guidance: "Lord, if you want me to do this book, then you're going to have to open the doors and make it happen. But if you don't, or you don't like the way it seems to be going, then I pray that you would block it, so that it cannot happen, no matter how much I might want it to.'' I had prayed that prayer about the rally book, and it looked like we were getting our answer.

Of primary importance, if we were to do the book, was the complete cooperation of the WFJ staff, including authorization to go behind the scenes for background material, as well as free access to all the principals for multiple interviews, and above all, an attitude of trust that regarded us as allies, not adversaries. With anything less than 100% cooperation, we might as well not attempt it, and certainly we had no intention of going ahead anyway, with what could wind up critical or antagonistic: the body of Christ had already suffered from enough of that sort of internal dissension and strife, with one part of the body deliberately torpedoing another. That was the sort of poison for which hopefully Washington For Jesus was going to prove an antidote.

What we did not realize until later, indeed could not even have conceived of at the time, was that there were only three full-time paid employees on the WFJ staff! The Kansas City conference had had at least four times that number, working a full year in advance, and they had drawn only a twentieth of the number that WFJ was hoping for. John Gilman was so snowed under that he would shortly have four additional phone lines run into his house, with two assistants just to answser them. Our book project, so important to us, was but one of thirty or forty matters that he was simultaneously considering.

But none of this was known to us, back on Cape Cod. Finally,the day arrived that we came to the end of our patience. Dean had been trying all morning to get through to John, and we were ready to give up and go out to lunch, and revise our schedule, when I said to Dean: ''You might as well give it one more try.'' So he did — and got through.

All I could hear, of course, was Dean's side of the conversation, and from that, it wasn't going too well. Apparently, since our initial proposal, several other potential book projects had come on the scene and . . . .

I could feel myself getting angry, and I was glad Dean was

on the phone instead of me, because he obviously had the grace to remain calm. But I prayed then that if it really was God's will for us to work together with these men, He would intervene — right now. Almost immediately, the tenor of the conversation changed: Dean was now mainly listening, and nodding and occasionally interjecting a word of sympathy or encouragement. Incredible! For several minutes this went on, and then I heard him say: "Well, maybe the best thing is for us to come down there and meet with you all. That way, you can catch our spirit, and we yours, and if God wants us to work together, we'll know it." And with that, a date was agreed upon, and he hung up.

I stood there, speechless. After days and days of unproductive effort, suddenly it all seemed to be coming together! It was getting hard to deny that God really did want us involved.

On Sunday, March 2nd, at 1:00 PM, Dean and I left home to drive the two hours to Logan Airport. At 1:30 PM, the call came from the airlines that our 3:30 flight to Norfolk had been cancelled, due to a sudden, fierce blizzard that had blanketed the Tidewater area. Had that call come before we left, we would in all likelihood have scrubbed the mission entirely and might never have gone down there. But as it was, we drove on up to Boston, put the car in Park, Shuttle and Fly, and did not discover the cancellation until we arrived at the check-in counter.

At a loss to know what to do next, we prayed and decided to go on down to Washington, which was still open, and see what the situation looked like when we got there. If worse came to worst, we could spend the night in D.C., rent a car in the morning, and drive the four hours to Virginia Beach. Our appointment was for noon; with any luck, we could just make it. But getting on a flight to Washington that afternoon was going to require a bit of "luck"; with Norfolk closed and Washington threatened, hundreds of travel plans on that normally busy weekend afternoon were being thrown into total confusion. Well, Lord. . . and as it happened, we got the last two seats on a Washington flight.

When we got to National Airport, it was cold all right, but there was no snow to be seen anywhere. The blizzard had moved out to sea and Norfolk airport was estimating that it would be dug out and operational by 11:00 PM. Dean said that had the ring of wishful thinking to him, and sure enough, when we returned to the terminal in the morning, their revised estimate was 8:00 AM. I looked at Dean, and he shook his head: we couldn't take the chance. So we rented a car and started south on I-95.

And now the Old Boy started to work on me: if this was really God's will, how come it was becoming so hard to get there? Were we trying to force this meeting to happen? And if it was God's will, why had He picked this particular weekend to visit Norfolk with the worst winter storm they had seen in twenty years? But I said nothing to Dean, whose thoughts, I suspected, were going in similar directions. Actually, the drive down was really quite pleasant — sunny and clear, with no sign of snow. Nor did we see any, until we reached Richmond, and turned east on I-64. Here, there was snow piled along-side the interstate, but the highway itself had been plowed clear. We were making good time, and I was surprised to note that we were practically the only car on the road.

Our first sign that there had indeed been a blizzard came when we arrived at the entrance to the Hampton Roads tunnel. It was packed to the top with snow! In fact, snow had blasted several hundred yards into the tunnel, and they were only just now breaking through with a team of front-end loaders and clearing one southbound lane for traffic. We sat and watched as dump-truck after dump-truck was loaded with snow, and the opening was gradually enlarged. Finally, the flagman waved us through, along with the few other cars that had been waiting.

I tried to imagine what it would be like to be trapped inside the tunnel, with both ends blocked, and gave it up as a bad idea. When we emerged, we had to squint: a dazzling sheet of white covered everything. Drifts up to six feet were everywhere, and many of the access roads to I-64 were still closed. Cars, window-deep in snow, were abandoned in the middle of the street, kids were home from school — I switched on the radio, to see if I could pick up a local newscast.

"The Governor's office has asked this station to repeat the announcement of a curfew on all private vehicles, except four-wheel drive vehicles actively engaged in rescue work. If you have an emergency, call your local police station, and they will get a vehicle to you. . . ."

I looked at Dean, who shrugged: "We're almost there; there's not much point in stopping here and blocking the snow removal."

I smiled wanly. "No wonder there was no traffic."

The newscast went on to tell of some 2300 people who, despite heavy snow warnings and being urged to stay home, had nonetheless gone to the circus in nearby Scope auditorium on Sunday afternoon. The snow was already falling thickly when they reached the auditorium parking lot, and by the time they came out, after the performance, the parking lot was completely snowbound. They had had to spend the night in the auditorium and were unable to leave until ten o'clock the following morning.

Fortunately, the Rock Church was located on one of the major access roads to I-64, which was cleared. We were able to get right to the church, although we couldn't get into the parking lot, which was being cleared by a crew of volunteer workers who had shown up for that purpose. Inside the modern circular structure, down in one of the basement offices, we met a brave young lady named Janet Keim who was manning the switchboard. She called John Gilman at home, to let him know that two men from Cape Cod had arrived at the church for their appointment with him, and she informed us that he would be on his way over, on foot, before too long. She also told us that the Governor's office had requested that no outgoing long-distance calls be made, or incoming long-distance business be conducted, unless it was an absolute emergency. As a result, the phones were quieter than they had been in months.

While waiting for John Gilman to trudge over, Dean and I took the opportunity to look around the church, which was truly impressive. We learned that there were some four thousand active members of the church, which meant three services were needed on Sundays, as the sanctuary sat only three thousand. I was particularly interested in the design of the sanctuary, because it did not seem that large to me; in fact, it had an almost cosy feeling to it. It was built like an amphitheatre, with seating in a 120° wedge of a circle, with a raised platform down front — or rather, *up* front, since the aisles went up an incline to the pulpit. This, I discovered, enabled the balcony to come much closer to the pulpit, with those in the front row of the balcony just slightly above the eye level of the preacher, instead of many feet above and away, as in a conventional balcony or choir loft. The result, as I was to experience later, was an extraordinary sense of closeness — and family — that I had nowhere else known in sanctuaries of less than a third the capacity of that one.

We went back to the church pantry and chatted with some of the maintenance men, who were warming up and taking a coffee break before going back to snow removal. We learned that there were twenty-seven other Rock Churches, which were, in a sense, spin-offs — churches that had started as a result of the spirit in this one. They were all independent from this one, but there was obviously a close bond of fellowship; in all, quite a remarkable testimony to the ministry of John Gimenez and his wife Anne, who had been there only twelve years. John himself had grown up in a New York ghetto, gotten involved in drugs, and served time in several penitentiaries before God reached out and called him. The details, we were told, were narrated in an exciting book called *Upon This Rock* by Robert Paul Lamb, which was available through the church.

"Hi, I'm John Gilman." We looked up to see a young man with a big grin, and a shock of hair down over his forehead. He was sensibly dressed in old dungarees, with saran-wrap taped around his ankles, and suddenly I felt more than a little over-dressed, in a three-piece business suit. But John didn't seem to notice, and Dean was unconcerned, as we sat down around the pantry table. We joked about all the snow, and then John came right to the point. Looking me in the eye, he asked me: "Why do you want to write this book?"

I started to say all the right things — and soon realized that I was not getting through. So I decided to tell him the truth: how much I *didn't* want to write the book. I told him about the novel, and how much I would have preferred to be in Bermuda right now, working on it. And then Dean told him about the scene in the Edwardian Room of the Plaza, and John laughed. Apparently, he, too, knew what it meant to have had one's heart set on one thing, only to have God send down a change in marching orders.

Things went well, after that. John excused himself and returned with a beautiful poster for Washington For Jesus, depicting a sculpture of Washington on one knee, praying. And not long after that, someone singing to himself in the corridor came wandering in, a short, dark fellow, wearing an old, once-white fisherman's-knit sweater that covered a fairly ample girth. I assumed he was one of the snow removal men, in from shoveling and looking for a cup of hot coffee.

John Gilman stood up and introduced John Gimenez. I got to my feet, and we shook hands all around. And then the four of us talked for two solid hours, without interruption. As we did, I began to appreciate God's infinite wisdom, and to repent for my own unbelief. This day, with all its snow, was probably the one day in the whole year in which John Gimenez spent the entire afternoon in the church, without having a single visitor, or a single phone call. Most of the time, he was on the road, telling people across the country about the rally. And on those rare occasions when he could actually be found in the church, his schedule was crammed with appointments, and there was usually a queue of people in his outer office waiting to have just a quick word with him, and a constant stream of incoming long-distance calls. And John being John, it was not his nature to cut anyone off. That we had two peaceful, relaxed, uninterrupted hours together, less than two months before the rally, was a miracle. And when it was over, we prayed together as new brothers in the Lord.

For all intents and purposes, we had the agreement for which we had come, although, as it turned out later, there were still some details that needed to be cleared up. We needed to get together again, and fortunately an event was coming up that would provide the perfect opportunity. On Tuesday, March 11th, Washington For Jesus had scheduled a national press conference in Washington, at which their steering committee would formally introduce the rally to the media, and answer any queries they might have. No one from WFJ had suggested that we come, and that surprised us, since it would make an obvious advance chapter for the book. We both felt the need to go and see where we stood, and so we called and made arrangements to meet with John Gilman afterwards.

The conference was to take place in the quiet, dignified University Club on 16th Street, a few blocks north of the White House. We got there early, and were welcomed by a young fellow named Ron Boehme, the Washington coordinator for Youth With A Mission, which organization would be providing many of the youth volunteers so vital to the success of the rally.

Informed that the steering committee was still in a private breakfast meeting, Dean and I went down to the reading room on the main floor, to wait until 10:00, when the conference was to begin. The reading room, with its attractive floor-to-ceiling shelves, and broad tables with magazines laid out, was quiet and inviting. It was also empty, and Dean and I ensconced ourselves in two corner chairs. Ron had given us a press kit, and now we sifted through the material, reading the various releases and updates, as well as a cogent interview with John Gimenez which succinctly recapped how the rally had come to pass.

Pastor Gimenez, what is Washington For Jesus?

It is the fulfillment of a vision the Lord gave us of His people reclaiming the government of this nation for Jesus Christ. It is a day — Tuesday, April 29, 1980 — set apart to call God's people to repentance.

At first, we saw it mainly as a day of praise and worship to the Lord, an affirmation that God still has a people, and that they are concerned about the direction of this nation and its government. Praise and worship will still play a big part in Washington For Jesus. It will be thrilling to join with thousands upon thousands of believers in adoration of our living Lord there on the Mall! To declare the Lordship of Jesus before a watching world.

But as we worked and prayed in the past months, God expanded our understanding of what He wants to do, of what He wants of us, the Church of Jesus Christ.

How do you envision Washington For Jesus now?

Now we see that God would have us come unto Him as the united Body of Christ and acknowledge our sinfulness: our neglect, our pride, our divisions, our lukewarmness, our compromise — all those things that interrupt our fellowship with Jesus.

We see that He is calling us to repentance. And of course, inherent in repentance is a turning away from sin and back to righteousness, to God. . . .

Many Congressmen and Senators have urged us as Christians

to take a stand for God, to wrest back the nation from the forces of unrighteousness. "We are at a point in America now, that it's either God, or chaos, ruin," one Senator said. A Congressman warned that by the mid-1980's, America will face internal subversion, bankruptcy, or military defeat. Another Senator asked us to pray that God won't permit any enemy to strike this continent, because we are not able to defend ourselves.

God has allowed all kinds of problems and crises, to cause us to turn to Himself. About the only thing we haven't seen yet is the wrath of God come upon this country, God's judgment of sin. And it is certain to come, unless God's people repent — *turn* — and intercede before God for the land. A righteous and holy God cannot forever tolerate the continued flaunting of His ways. We see example after example of this in His dealings with the children of Israel.

But we have God's promise that when His people come to Him in genuine sorrow for their disobedience, as God tells us in II Chronicles 7:14, they humble themselves and pray and seek God's face, and turn from their wicked ways, then He *will* hear from heaven, and *will* forgive their sins, and *will* heal their land.

That's the covenant of a holy God with us. We have His word. And He is faithful and true to His word. God can hold off His judgment on this generation.

How does Washington For Jesus fit into this?

It is a day of humiliation, prayer and fasting, a day of turning — individually and corporately — from our sin, to righteousness.

The Lord burdened us with this vision of the prophet Joel, which is a warning of God to a demoralized society, with its parallels for us. We came to see that God wants His people to feel what He is feeling — grief over sin — and that on April 29th, God wants contrition and tears flowing, hearts broken because of sin. We believe God is speaking to His church today through Joel, when He tells His people to "sound an alarm," because His judgment is "near at hand." He commands that they repent, that they "set apart a fast — a day of restraint and humility. Call a solemn assembly, gather the people. . . and cry unto the Lord."

What are God's conditions?

We saw them in II Chronicles 7:14, and God restates them in Joel 2:12 and 13 — "Therefore also now, says the Lord, turn and keep on coming to me with all your heart, with fasting, with weeping, and with mourning, until every hindrance is removed and broken fellowship is restored. Rend your hearts and not your garments, and return to the Lord your God."

In the book of Zephaniah, Chapter 2, we see God commanding repentance "before the fierce anger of the Lord comes upon you." He tells His people in verse 3 to "seek the Lord," to require Him as the foremost necessity of your life. The Amplified Bible puts it: "to seek righteousness, seek humility — inquire for them, require them as vital." And "it may be that you will be hidden in the day of the Lord's anger."

When God orders the gathering of His people in Joel, no one is exempt. He says to include the elderly, the children, the nursing infants, even the newly married. And his ministers — He tells His ministers to weep before Him as they intercede, that God might spare His people.

Joel tells us that God heard the cries of repentance and "had pity on His people." He poured out material blessings upon them, He turned away their enemies, He caused their land to be fruitful, and He was in the midst of them. Those were the fruits of returning and repentance.

What was the genesis for Washington For Jesus?

God began to speak to us about bringing His people to Washington, D.C. during a Bible conference in California in July, 1978. I was preaching from I Samuel 17, the story of David and Goliath, and David asks, "Is there not a cause?" God began to show that there *is* a cause, a message. Even as in that day, a Goliath was seeking to destroy Israel, today a Goliath seeks to destroy the very foundations of the American system that once was totally based on the Word of God. Even as David aimed at Goliath's head and slew him, so we have to go to the capital —

the head of government — where unrighteousness is being legislated.

At the outset, God showed me that He would confirm that this was His program, that His favor was on it. And He has, through many brothers. The men God led me to also felt that this was God's timing, and that if something is to reverse the trend of the nation away from God, it must be done now! Since then, many have joined the growing ranks of spiritual leaders who are hearing from God that this is our last chance.

We have seen miracles take place, as God has moved to overcome obstacles and bring together many segments within His church — blacks and whites, fundamentalists, charismatics and evangelicals, Catholics and Protestants. . . .

What miracles have you seen?

Perhaps the greatest miracle we've witnessed has been the coming together of the Body of Christ, the putting aside of doctrinal differences. Not compromise or concession, but conciliation and consensus around the person of Jesus Christ, our common Savior.

There have been miracles of a practical nature, too. For instance, the logistical plan that God provided. In advance of the Pope's visit last October, the planners in Washington put together this tremendous plan to cover every contingency in dealing with a million visitors — only they didn't get to test it fully, because they didn't have that many people. So, they passed it along to us. . . .

How would you summarize what you hope to achieve?

We have a three-fold purpose: to minister to God, to minister to the nation and government, and to minister to the Body of Christ, His Church.

How?

By calling believers from every part of the Church together in heart-rending repentance before Almighty God, and in intercession for this nation. We desire this, not simply that we might

be spared as a nation, but because the nature of a holy and just
God demands it. Because our sinfulness demands it.

God's forgiveness and restoration — His sparing us from
judgment — are fruits of true repentance. But sorrow for our sin
is the only basis for repentance, not our desire to avoid judgment. And sorrow for sin comes only as we come into the presence of God, as we see Him as He is, and ourselves as we are, in
His pure light. That's when the turning will come, and along
with it, God's forgiveness and His healing for our land.

*Heart-rending repentance. . . sorrow for our sin, as the only basis of
repentance. . . coming to see ourselves as we are* — these were strong
words for this day and age, and not the sort of thing you would
expect to hear from the average charismatic preacher, even the
more prominent ones. But then, I was beginning to become
aware that there was nothing average about John Gimenez.

There was one more piece in the press kit, which I just had
time to read before we went back upstairs. It was a preamble,
which began with a quotation from an earlier proclamation of a
day of fasting, humiliation and prayer:

> We have been recipients of the choicest bounties of heaven; we
> have grown in numbers, wealth and power as no other nation
> has ever grown. But we have forgotten God. We have vainly
> imagined in the deceitfulness of our hearts that all these blessings
> were produced by some superior wisdom and virtue of our own.
> Intoxicated with unbroken success, we have become too self-
> sufficient to feel the necessity of redeeming grace. Too proud to
> pray to the God who made us.''

The date at the bottom of the proclamation was April 30,
1863, and the signature was Abraham Lincoln's. My mind
went back to the face carved in white marble in the memorial,
and the grief in those watching eyes. . . .

Dean nudged me; it was time to go upstairs.

John Gimenez

Pat Robertson

Bill Bright

Ted and Louise Pantaleo

John and Caroline Gilman

John Jones

Francis Owen in the transportation command center

John Sorensen

Bart Pierce   Cush Dobbs

Jerry Kantowski

Dan Ford

David Manuel

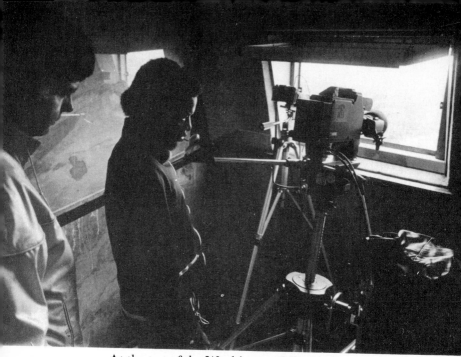

At the top of the Washington Monument

Dean Smith
and
John French

Ev Sahrbeck

Luke Norman and Paul Moore

Shirley Boone

Iverna Tompkins

Dale Evans Rogers

Sarah Jordan Powell

Ann Gimenez

Ann Kiemel

Pat Robertson and Fr. Michael Scanlan

Bishop Patterson

David DuPlessis

Bishop Williams

James Robison

Fritz Klein as the 16th President

Larry Tomczak

Bishop Winley

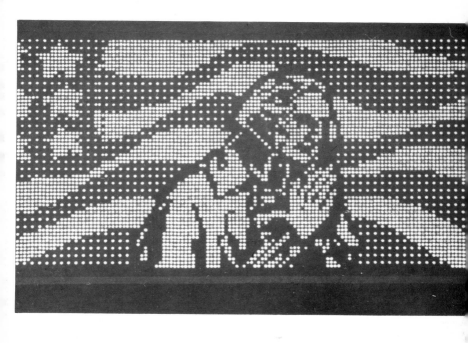

View from the press room

Arthur Blessitt

4

Meet the Press

The large, paneled reception room was transformed by powerful, portable spotlights on high poles, giving the speakers' podium the high-intensity lighting required by television cameras. They also gave the long, felt-covered steering committee table the appearance of a Senate investigation about to get underway. Folding chairs were set up facing the table for the more than ninety press representatives who had been invited, and a CBN camera crew was making some final lighting adjustments, while someone else was checking out the mike at the podium.

Dean and I took two seats at the back of the room and a little to one side, in order to leave the designated folding chairs for the legitimate members of the press. Just then, a familiar face disengaged itself and came over and joined us — this was Ronn Kerr, of Kerr Associates, who had handled the press relations in Kansas City in 1977, and whom we had recommended to John Gilman and John Gimenez down in Virginia Beach. Ronn told us that he had been invited as an observer and assumed that he and they would be making up their minds about each other that day. In the meantime, I was grateful for his being there, because he was able to point out who was who among the press people, as they now began to filter in. In all, twenty-four came — a disappointing turnout, I felt, since most of those present were from religious media. But Ronn assured me that both wire services were represented, and the Washington *Star* had sent a reporter.

Promptly at 10:30, the door at the end of the room opened, and the steering committee filed in and took their places at the table. I was surprised to see that at least half of the dozen men representing the steering committee were dressed in dark blue, three-piece suits, looking for all the world like Wall Street bankers. The contrast between their apparel and that of the press corps could not have been more acute. In their own way, the members of the press were conforming to their ideal even more so: their clothes were studiously casual, even scruffy, as if to let it be known that they were totally independent and singularly unimpressed with society's conception of a well-groomed appearance.

The conference had already gotten under way, with the deputy mayor concluding his welcoming remarks, when a tall, angular, middle-aged woman, dressed in slacks, a blazer and high heels, and smoking a cigarette, entered and took a seat in the back row of the folding chairs. "Marjorie Hyer," whispered Ronn, "the Washington *Post*'s lead religion writer."

John Gimenez, as chairman of the steering committee, was the first to speak. He told them briefly of the camp meeting in California, where he had first shared his growing sense of a need for a national rally of Christians, and how they had enthusiastically received it and appointed him chairman. He had laughed, too, but he also sensed that God was saying something to them, and in succeeding days, as he prayed about it, he couldn't get it out of his mind and out of his heart. The Lord seemed to place two names before him: Pat Robertson, president of the Christian Broadcasting Network, and Demos Shakarian, founder and president of the Full Gospel Businessmen's Fellowship, International.

He went to see Pat three times, he said, because for Pat,

being a lawyer by background, it took that long to really get the message across. Finally, at the end of their third meeting, he said, "Pat, you know that if a multitude, a hundred thousand of us gathered there, that would be a tremendous thing, a tremendous witness of all backgrounds, all denominations, all colors and races, coming together in an expression of love, a once-in-a-lifetime celebration of the Lordship of Jesus Christ. And the only thing that is going to affect this nation is when the Church begins to demonstrate the unity of Jesus Christ in our midst."

At that, Pat had looked up from the piece of paper that he was writing on and said, "John, I really feel this *is* of God. There's only one thing wrong with what you're saying: if there are only a hundred thousand Christians out there who are concerned enough about this nation to do something, to gather, to try to change the course that our country is on, then we're in trouble!" He thought for a moment and then added, "If five thousand pastors brought two hundred people each, that would be a million right there!" And that was how they had begun believing for a million people.

John went on to tell about his meeting with Demos Shakarian. It took place during one of Demos' visits to Washington, in the latter's hotel room at the Shoreham. It was 2:00 AM, and John had been talking to him about the rally for almost two hours. Demos had still not made up his mind, and finally John got up to leave. At the door, he turned and said, "Demos, I know the Lord spoke to me, to go to Pat and you for confirmation, and frankly, I'm perfectly happy to just go on pastoring my church. If you say that you don't sense God in this, I'll go home and forget the whole thing."

Instead of replying, Demos had taken him by the arm and led him back into the room. "John," he said slowly, "I feel that it could be of God, but let me take it back to my leaders." He did, and for the first time in their history, the Full Gospel Businessmen voted unanimously to back a project that was entirely outside of their own ministry. Their support, like CBN's, was to prove crucial in the ensuing months, for their thousand-plus chapters functioned as information-disseminating centers, without which Washington For Jesus could never have gotten the word out as far as it had.

"Since then," John concluded, "it has been nothing short of miraculous how God has moved and touched and begun to unite people from different backgrounds, people who theologically perhaps have differences, but who have unity in Christ Jesus."

The next person to step to the podium was Pat Robertson, co-chairman of the program committee. He led off by quoting something that Walter Cronkite had said four years ago: "There can be no doubt that history is at a turning point, and we are suffering around the world with what one philosopher has called a civilizational malaise and an unidentified uneasiness. The question is: are we at the end of a civilization, facing a new dark age like the Romans were? Or are we at the beginning of a new Renaissance? The problems are immense, gargantuan, so great that on their solution depends whether we live or die — at the very least, what quality of life we will have. It is a gloomy moment in the history of our country. Not in the life of most men has there been such grave and deep apprehension. Never has the future seemed so incalculable as at this time."

Pat looked at the assembled journalists. "What Mr. Cronkite said in 1976 has been exacerbated in the last four years. It is my personal feeling that the United States and western civilization are entering, the next two or three years, a period of maximum peril, politically, financially and militarily. Our entire society and civilization is in the balance. The spectre of war has been raised in a Presidential speech. There has been a brutal invasion of Afghanistan. Our hostages are still being held in Iran. There is chaos in the currency market. . . .

"And now we are coming to Washington, hopefully one

million strong. . . . We are coming to offer no legislative program. We are coming to support no candidate whatsoever in any part for public office. Instead, we are coming as representatives of the body of Jesus Christ, in as broad a spectrum as we can. For speakers we're having Hispanics, we're having blacks, we're having Roman Catholics, we're having Lutherans, Methodists, Southern Baptists, Pentecostals, charismatics, evangelicals — people from as broad a religious life as you can find who will gather with us and repent of our corporate sins as Christians, and ask God to forgive us.''

It was time for Pat's conclusion, and he put it as plainly as he could: ''We're looking for a healing in the United States of America. We're faced with virtually insoluble problems. And we're going to call on the God of our fathers to enter into the stream of history and to take charge and bring His mercy and His grace and His protection and His deliverance to our land, and to our world.'' He paused. ''It is our feeling that it's either Christ, or chaos.''

I looked at the reporters and was disappointed to note that none of them were taking notes, for Pat had said some eminently quotable things. He then introduced his co-chairman on the program committee, Dr. Bill Bright, founder and director of Campus Crusade for Christ International, which had a staff of 11,500 regular and associate members, serving in 114 countries throughout the world. I had seen Bill Bright before, and from a distance he had struck me as a reserved man, cautious about what he said and possessing a quiet dignity that commanded respect. It was still a surprise to think of him involving himself, and his friends among the evangelical leadership, in what had started out to be a charismatic project, and I listened with interest to what he would have to say.

''I'd like to mention some of the Scriptural and logical reasons why we are coming to Washington for a day of prayer,'' he said in matter-of-fact, businesslike tones. ''First, we believe that there is a God in heaven. We believe that God is a God of love. And He loves men of all nations, cultures, and creeds. We believe that God is holy, righteous and just. We believe that the Bible teaches, and history confirms, that when individuals and nations obey God, He blesses. And when they disobey God, He punishes, chastening them just as faithful parents discipline their children — because they love them, not because they hate them.

"I'd like to call your attention to a couple of examples of this in Deuteronomy 8 and 28, where God says to His people Israel: 'If you obey me, I will bless you,' and He proceeds to list all the many blessings that would be poured out on Israel. Then He says: 'If you disobey me, here is what will happen,' and a list follows of all the acts of chastening. And in the Book of Amos, chapter 4, God says to Israel: 'In a way of trying to get your attention, I sent hunger, but you didn't listen to me. I ruined your crops by holding back the rain, but you still wouldn't come to me. I sent blight and mildew to your farms and your vineyards, and locusts ate your figs and olive trees, but you still wouldn't return to me. And I killed your young men in war and drove away your horses, and you still wouldn't listen to me. I destroyed some of your cities, and you still would not listen to me.' ''

And now Dr. Bright went on to make a comment that took quite a bit of courage. "I believe that in 1962, something incredible happened in our nation, a nation that was built upon the Scriptures, and that for more than three hundred years had most of its schools established as Christian schools where, along with the fundamentals, basic Biblical truths were taught. In 1962, the highest court in our land declared that prayer no longer had any place in our schools. Let us consider what happened then, just as in the days of Israel. Almost immediately after that decision, there was the assassination of President Kennedy, and the nation was plunged into mourning. The student revolution of the '60's followed, then the assassination of Senator Kennedy, and the assassination of

Martin Luther King. Crime increased over 300% in those immediate years. The tragedy of Vietnam almost destroyed our nation. The drug revolution did destroy the lives of countless thousands of our young people and influenced the lives of many millions more. There was the disintegration of the homes of America, racial conflict in city after city, and a political scandal that shook our nation.

"Some might choose to think of these things as mere happenings, but I believe they were plagues — plagues that continue today, because of our continued disobedience to God. For example, we are plagued with an epidemic of teenage pregnancies, an epidemic of venereal disease, an epidemic of drug addiction, an epidemic of alcoholism — the list goes on almost endlessly. God is still trying to get our attention, as He did with Israel and Judah both.

"And now, finally, we are faced with one of the most dramatic moments in the history of civilization, with the very threat of nuclear destruction a real possibility, and the possibility that we, as a nation, could lose our lives and our freedom.

"And so we come to Washington, our nation's capital, in the spirit of men and women who know that we have sinned. As individuals, as believers, we've disobeyed God. We'll be asking God to accept our confession, our repentance, and heal our land. . . .

"If there is a God, and there is — if He loves us, and He does — if we disobey, He chastens us. And if we confess our sins, He forgives and heals." And with that statement, he had reached his conclusion: "We believe that there is great logic and Scriptural basis for this gathering, which could be the most important day in the history of our nation."

As Dr. Bright sat down, I thought about what he had said about the plagues. It seemed to me that he was hanging too much on the Supreme Court decision banning prayer in schools, but I was nonetheless intrigued by his stringing together of the "happenings" which followed in its wake. Certainly in *The Light and the Glory,* Peter Marshall and I had also pegged 1963 as the year that America finally tilted over the precipice and began its accelerating toboggan ride down into the morass of chaos, lapping below. . . . I again glanced around at the press, but none of them seemed to be responding.

Ted Pantaleo, national coordinator for Washington For Jesus, spoke next: "Eighteen months ago, we began one of the most fascinating adventures I've ever been a part of. I was sent to Washington to start work on the permits we would need, and then I traveled across the land, talking to the grass roots leaders on all levels in every state. At the same time, in our own headquarters, we began developing logistical teams for everything from medical emergency services to telephone communications to assigning security personnel. Because Pat Robertson said one thing at the outset, which I'm not even sure he remembers." He grinned over at Pat. *"Bathe it in prayer and take care of your logistics.* And that's what we've tried to do. For the past year and a half we have traveled everywhere, talking to blacks, whites, Hispanics, denominational and non-denominational folks, setting up leadership for state coordinators, women coordinators, youth coordinators, prayer coordinators, you name it. And now it is happening, and they're coming to Washington — more than a hundred thousand are already committed, and I believe that we'll see many, many more make the commitment in the weeks that remain."

At this point, those other members of the steering committee who were present were introduced: Dr. Charles Keysor, founder and editor of the bi-monthly magazine *Good News* and a popular leader of the evangelical movement within the United Methodist Church; James Robison, the crusade evangelist whose ninety-minute telecasts were seen weekly on more than one hundred stations; Ben Haden, the soft-spoken pastor of the First Presbyterian Church in Chattanooga, Tennessee, who was regularly seen and heard on the TV and radio program, "Changed Lives"; Demos Shakarian; Bishop Jesse Winley, the old but still fiery black founder and president of the Soul Saving Stations, a dynamic inner-city ministry, head-quartered in Harlem; Raimundo Jimenez from El Paso, who with his brother had preached at the largest Latin American crusades of any Hispanic evangelist.

John Gilman then opened the meeting for questions, and not surprisingly the first was: would the President be coming?

I recalled then, that despite his decision not to make public appearances during the hostage crisis, in February he had managed to slip over to the Washington Hilton to address the NRB convention there. The meeting was told that yes, the President had been invited to the rally, and it was very much hoped that he would come. But if he did, he would be coming as a private citizen, to join the rest of those present in prayer. For neither he, nor any other politician — and every Senator and Congressman would shortly be receiving a personal invita-tion — would be asked to speak to those gathered on the Mall that day.

Next, one of the wire service reps, with an untamed afro haircut, spoke up. "There is a document going around that purports to be some sort of declaration of intent and has a number of specific concerns on it — if not outright support — given to legislation on school prayer and abortion, among other things. I left a copy of it on my desk, because I expected it to be in here," he said, gesturing at the press kit he had been given, "but I see that it isn't. What is the status of that document?"

There was some hesitation among the steering committee, and I sat up in my chair. I, too, had heard rumors of such a declaration; was it on this document that the press was basing its new assertions regarding WFJ? For some stories were beginning to claim that the whole movement was political, nothing but the New Right, wrapping itself in the banner of Christianity, rather than the American flag.

Finally, Pat Robertson stood up. "I'll speak to that," he

said. "Whatever may have been circulating was a preliminary draft. It is the feeling of the steering committee that the emphasis should be on God, as opposed to politics. In the event that the political process impinges on certain religious activities and freedoms, the concern of Christian people might be expressed. However, it is being expressed *not* in a political context, but in a moral context. The steering committee is meeting today, and that particular document that you're referring to is undergoing a rather substantial revision at this time."

The wire service man pursued his point. "Well, if it's not political, would you explain the intercessory prayer lists for Congress that are going to be brought?"

Ted Pantaleo came to the microphone. "What we are attempting to do is get a thousand people from the home district of each Congressman, who are willing to pray for him every day. We've set this up under Dr. Warren Singleton, an intercessory prayer warrior from our church. We have a special team back at Washington For Jesus headquarters on the phones all the time, contacting churches and intercessory prayer groups around the country. On April 28th, we hope to have a thousand people from each district signed up, so that we can present these lists to the Congressmen."

There were several other questions after that, but I was waiting to see what, if anything, Marjorie Hyer would ask. Of all the papers in the country, the *Post* would be the most closely watched for its reaction to WFJ; indeed, other journalists who weren't present themselves would be paying particular attention to see how she wrote her story. And after the others had finished asking their questons, she raised her finger.

John Gilman nodded to her, and she asked, "What is your overall, total budget for this operation?"

"We've had to revise it continuously," John replied, "because John Gimenez started by asking the people of his own church to help, and relying on the faith that it was available. We have figures being worked on at this very moment that will better be able to answer that later. If we gave out any figures now, they'd have to be adjusted.''

But Ms. Hyer was not that easily put off. ''But what's the current figure?'' she insisted. ''Surely you must have some sort of budget figure?''

John Gilman did not feel he was authorized to comment further, and so he looked over at John Gimenez, who rose and paused for a moment before he spoke. I could imagine what was going through his mind: If this woman was determined to do a torpedo job on Washington For Jesus, no matter what figure he named or what kind of explanation he made, it would not satisfy her or make a bit of difference. So, in that instant, he decided on full disclosure: ''I think,'' he said, proceeding slowly, ''that we have spent up to this point, in the year and a half that we have been working, about 150 to 160 thousand dollars. By the time it is all over, our ballpark figure will be somewhere between 750 thousand and a million dollars. But we have had so much voluntary help and contributions towards the work — the use of presses, and that sort of thing — do you know that we have only three people full-time on the payroll?''

That apparently took care of it, and now another reporter asked what sort of media coverage they were hoping to get. Ben Haden answered that one. ''I think it is important to say that this is *not* a media event,'' he said quietly. ''We're interested, of course, in the participation of Christians across the country. Our major purpose is not media coverage, but to come before God, because we believe in prayer. We believe there is no media coverage whatever in one's relationship with God, in the act of prayer.''

Now John Gimenez arose again, with an addendum to his answer to Ms. Hyer's question: ''Another reason why our budget is very low is that we have had no real financial campaign to raise funds. In fact, it is sort of a miraculous story just how we have gotten this far. And a third reason is that there are no paid personalities coming; everyone will be paying his own way. People like Pat Boone and other nationally-known entertainers are doing this for the Lord first and then for the nation, and so are coming at their own expense. One group of musicians, coming from California, will spend fifteen thousand dollars of their own money to travel to Washington, but that's how important it is to all of us. It will be a sacrifice for many. We know of people who are coming from Hawaii, who will be spending $600 per person, just to be there.'' He looked at her and the others, his palms open. ''We're saying, 'We love this country. We know that the only answer is in Christ, and that's why we're coming.' First of all, we'll be there to ask the Lord to forgive us as Christians, for our complacency and division, and then to ask Him to heal our land. And we have to do it, because we love the Lord.''

I felt like applauding. But the press, their notebooks already put away, looked bored and grateful that it was over. They left quickly.

No matter, I thought; enough was said this morning so that if they heard only a third or a quarter of it, it couldn't help but make a good story. And I was glad John Gilman had had the prescience to schedule it for Tuesday, so that they would have plenty of time to work it into a major piece for the weekend papers, if they chose to. All things considered, I felt it had gone as well as could possibly have been hoped for. It was a shame there weren't more newsmen there, but I was confident that the rally would get the positive send-off in the media that they were hoping for.

Which only showed that for someone who prided himself on his astuteness, I was incredibly naive.

5

Unto God, or
Unto Caesar?

As the press conference broke up into small informal groups, Dean and I took the opportunity to talk with Ted Pantaleo, the national coordinator, because there were suddenly several large questions I wanted to ask him, but not in front of the press. For instance, where on earth were they going to put several hundred thousand overnight visitors? I had learned that the Arizona contingent, coming in two buses, expected to be staying in Harrisonburg, Virginia, a good two hours' drive away, because those were the nearest accommodations that they could get. Admittedly, they had started late, but where did that leave all those who wouldn't get around to making their arrangements until the last three or four weeks? And also, wouldn't that many people, all coming in to Washington at the same time, do a job on their transportation system?

For a moment the smile on Ted's perpetually cheerful visage sagged. It was obvious that these were hardly new considerations; in fact, he had probably been thinking about little else for weeks. But then he took a deep breath, the smile came back, and he explained. "We have made a concerted effort to ask people in Virginia and the close-by eastern states, to come and go in the same day and leave the hotel rooms for people coming from across the country. Also, many of the families in local churches will be opening their homes to fellow Christians from far away. But one of our big objectives is to get people into the city *before* the 29th, because I'm afraid the city is going to be pretty well glutted with traffic on the day of the rally, and we want to lessen that impact as much as possible." He shook his head at the thought of what it was going to be like. "As a matter of fact, we are asking people, through pulpits and newspapers and everywhere, for those coming not to drive into Washington at all that day. If they will take the Metro, that's our subway, into the Mall, that will help alleviate congestion."

But wouldn't that just be removing the traffic jam one step, farming it out to the suburbs, as it were?

"Not necessarily. We are going to be asking locals to stay on the Mall until after five, to give the out-of-towners a chance to leave early."

It did seem to me, that if God *was* raising up this rally, and it seemed that He was, then His Spirit would go before, and would ensure that traffic flowed smoothly; indeed, that might be one of the biggest surprises of all.

Just then Demos Shakarian, recognizing my partner Dean from earlier years, came over and gave him a hearty greeting. I asked Demos what he himself thought was the single most important aspect of the forthcoming rally, and without hesitation he replied: *"Unity.* Christians returning from South America have told me that if the Church there had been together, according to the prayer of Jesus, and had the people in South America seen this unity, the things that were happening in so many countries down there wouldn't have happened. The falling apart of nations and the growing trend towards Communism — this wouldn't have happened, had the Christians *worked together.* The people saw more unity among the Communists than they did among the Christians, and they had expected more of the Christians than they had of the

Communists. But when they don't see it, they can't believe it or accept it.''

Demos shook his head. ''That's why unity, coming together and working together as a body, is so important. We can be apart doctrinally, but spiritually we have got to have more unity. And this is what Washington For Jesus is doing. If it has an impact — and I believe it will, that we are ready to see the prayer of Jesus answered — this could be the most important act in this time, one that could change the destiny of America.''

We were left with that thought, as people began to go their separate ways for lunch. John Gilman had invited us to come over to the Shoreham, where the WFJ people were staying, to have lunch with him in his room, and to iron out the few remaining wrinkles in our arrangement. When we got there, and had compared notes about how the conference had gone, I asked John about the document to which the wire service reporter had referred. John produced a copy of it, in the form of a mailing piece that had already gone out to a great many people, and added that, up until that morning, they had planned to carry it as one of the pages of the newspaper supplement that they were then in the process of putting together. But, as we had heard at the conference, the steering committee had taken exception to much of the wording of the declaration, and so it was being substantially revised.

I glanced at it, noted that it was called ''A Christian Declaration'' and was too long to read then, and I stuck it in my brief case. For just then there was a knock at the door, and John Gimenez joined us. Once more, we enjoyed an unexpected and uninterrupted hour together, while everyone else was downstairs in the busy dining room. It was enough time to get everything wrapped up, and when John Gimenez had to leave and we shook hands, it was to seal a complete agreement.

John apologized for having to leave, but, he explained, he and Demos and Bishop Winley had an appointment with Mark

Hatfield, and they couldn't take a chance on the mid-day traffic making them late. We wished him well; of all the Christians on the Hill, Senator Hatfield was probably the best known. His endorsement of the rally would be a boon. In the meantime, Dean and I had a plane to catch back to Boston. We thanked John Gilman for the lunch and agreed that we would all keep in closer touch.

I did not get a chance to look at the declaration until that evening, as we were waiting at Logan airport for the shuttle flight to Hyannis. Dean and I read it together. It started off with the same preamble as was in the press kits, quoting Lincoln and II Chronicles 7:14 — so far so good. It wasn't until it got down to Article III that it began to get heavy.

We call upon this nation to repent of conduct contrary to the purposes for which it was founded and the clear commandment of the Word of God:

1. There is adultery, rape, fornication, homosexuality, and filthiness of mind through the land.

2. Lying, stealing, drunkenness and murder are rampant. We prey upon one another. Our streets are full of bloodshed and violence. Official corruption abounds.

3. Homes are destroyed by divorce. Unions other than holy matrimony are established between men and women. Parents neglect their young. The young do not honor their parents.

4. We slaughter our unborn infants on the altar of personal selfishness.

5. We allow pornographers and traffickers in drugs to force themselves upon our children. The truth of God is taken from our schools by action of government, while unbridled sexuality, humanism, and Satanism are taught at public expense.

6. The government has become bloated at the expense of its citizens. The servant has become our master. Freedom and initiative have been throttled by bureaucracy run wild.

7. Our currency has been debased, our elderly beggared by inflation. Our poor have become perpetual wards of the state and our armed forces weakened.

8. Our government has aided our enemies and destroyed our

friends. We have assisted the oppressors and weakened the victims. Government has encouraged the atheistic enemies of God, while often repressing the godly.

I let out a low whistle. "No wonder the media have begun to cast Washington For Jesus in a political light!" I looked at Dean. "In another context, these points might serve as the heart of a new Conservative Manifesto."

Dean did not respond. "Read the rest," he murmured.

The last Article was addressed to our elected representatives:

In these times of crisis, we pray God's wisdom and blessing upon you. We support you and uphold you. Yet we exhort you to remember that you are first servants of God, then servants of the people. Exalt the common good above personal and partisan concern. Refuse to be swayed by the clamor of self-seeking special-interest groups. Bear in mind that only God is the ultimate guarantor of the needs of our people — and when government usurps the role of God, it becomes tyranny. Lead our people in noble causes and do not be afraid to ask for sacrifice when the common good demands it. Frame laws, statutes, and ordinances that are in harmony with God's word. Be a model of honesty and truthfulness for those you lead. Glorify God by your life, your words and your public acts.

When I finished, I was in turmoil inside, and it took a few moments to sort out my different reactions. First of all, I wholeheartedly concurred with every one of the eight points listed in Article III. We had written essentially the same thing in *The Light and the Glory*; I had expressed the same sentiments before many audiences and had applauded them in sermons and editorials; and I certainly intended to vote in November in exact accordance with the concerns indicated.

But at the same time, I had deep misgivings about the tone and attitude of the declaration, if it was meant to speak for all of us who would gather on the Mall five weeks hence. In my spirit, I sensed that God intended for us to come there in a different heart attitude — in humility and repentance for our *own* sins. I had no objection to a Christian brother promulgating such a declaration as far and widely as possible; in fact, if it were in the form of a petition, I would gladly put my name to it and assist physically or financially in getting others to sign it as well. But it was not what I felt God wanted me to say that day we would gather on the Mall. For April 29th was God's day, and November 4th was Caesar's.

In its present form, I felt the declaration would actually have the reverse effect of that which its author or authors desired. For the instinctive response to pressure was resistance, no matter where the pressure was coming from (as those of us who had known God and nonetheless struggled against Him could attest). It seemed counter-productive to be calling one's unregenerate fellow citizens and elected representatives to repentance, let alone exhorting them to be "honest, sober and God-fearing" and lead more virtuous lives. For if one did not know the Lord, it was next to impossible for him to amend his life on the deep and meaningful level that was being called for. I had never known of anyone who had been coerced into moral rectitude, let alone into the Kingdom of God.

It seemed to me that we *could* appeal to non-believers, both in the capital and watching across the country, in many ways: we could witness to them in words and deeds, and even more tellingly in our living example. We could demonstrate our love for them and for one another, and our resolute determination to do everything that our Lord called us to do, to save the Republic. But if we came pointing our fingers and denouncing their behavior, we would come off as supremely self-righteous and would wind up putting off the very people that we hoped to attract to Jesus' cause.

But, oh, the temptation to take the opportunity to finally get a lick in at Caesar! Imagine the impact of a million *voting* Christians on the Mall! With the implication of forty or fifty more at home, for each one who actually came! Imagine the political clout, when one considered that only sixty-eight million Americans voted in the last election! The idealists had had it their way for too long! Well-organized, articulate and persuasive, they had wielded an influence far greater than their actual numbers, flattering the intellects of our young people, gradually taking control of the government, and ultimately almost ruining our country. And now, at last, we had an opportunity to redress the balance — a God-given opportunity — perhaps the last that aroused Christians would ever have. Delegations were going to be calling on the members of Congress anyway; why not take that opportunity to just go down their voting record and point out where they had voted in ways we felt were an affront to God? Talk about lobbying — Congress would never be the same!

But neither would our credibility. As tempting as such thinking was, if we gave in to it we would become a cartoon caricature of what we intended to be, lumped in the same bag with an axe-wielding Carrie Nation, busting up saloons at the turn of the century. And we would wind up being resented, even more than the angry, fist-in-the-air, bullhorn-chanting protest marchers of the Sixties — because we held ourselves to be better than they.

But if we did not yield to temptation, we might just gain *in*directly that very thing that we would hope to achieve in eyeball-to-eyeball confrontation. Assuming that at least 30% of American adults were already with us unshakably, no matter what the issue, from homosexual rights to abortion, it was probably realistic to assume that 30% was just as vehemently opposed and would not change their position, no matter how moving or persuasive our case might be. That meant there were 40% in the middle, who could go either way. For a long time, the other side had wooed this 40% and begun to take them for granted, while we had sat back passively and prayed that the Lord would deliver us the victory — or simply decided that politics was something that would somehow sully us

spiritually if we got involved in it. As a result, we often quit
the field before the contest, giving it to the other side by
default, to the point that they had even won over a number of
our own young people, so that now, in too many issues, they
had just about assured themselves of a majority.

So — what could we do? We could emulate Jesus Christ.
That was the one great force they did not have. And if He was
with us, then what did it matter who or what was against us?
Literally — with Him in our midst, nothing else mattered. If
we had the mind of Christ and His Spirit, if our repentance was
heartfelt, then would our joy and compassion be also, and He
would be the victor. It *could* happen — Demos had said our
unity could be the thing that could change the destiny of
America — but would it? It all depended on the spirit that
prevailed upon the Mall. . . would we render unto Caesar, or
unto God?

Dean jabbed me with his elbow. Our flight had just been
announced, and it was time to go to the gate. The trip in the
little two-engined commuter plane was the best kind —
uneventful — and before too long, we were back home. It was
not too late to call John Gilman, and Dean, who had been
working on some details on the plane, had a couple of things he
wanted to check out with him. He used the phone in our
kitchen, and when he was finished, I got on. "How did it go
with Senator Hatfield?"

There was a pause. "Not good," came the subdued reply.

"What happened?"

There was another pause. Then, "Well, you might as well
know: when John and Demos and Bishop Winley were shown
into his office, Dick Halverson and Doug Coe were also
there."

"Huh?" I couldn't imagine what the pastor of "Fourth
Pres," the most prestigious Presbyterian church in the D.C.
metro area, and the director of the low-key but influential
Fellowship House were doing there.

"John was a little surprised, too. They said, 'Do you still

maintain that your rally is non-political?' and he assured them that it was. 'Then how do you explain this?' Senator Hatfield asked, producing a letter he had just received. The letter was from one of our western coordinators.'' John fell silent again.

''What did it say?'' I made myself ask.

''Well, basically it was something like. . .'' and he para-phrased: ''This is to inform you that one million voters will be coming to Washington April 29th, and in conjunction with their coming, a delegation will be calling on you, to go over your voting record with you. These men will be reporting your response back to Christian voters in every Congressional district in your state.'' He paused again. ''There was more in the same vein.''

I groaned. The thing we feared the most had come upon us. ''What did John say?''

''There wasn't much he could say. He pointed out that the brother was acting entirely on his own initiative, and that no one in Washington For Jesus headquarters had any idea that he was contemplating such a thing. But that's not the worst part.''

I waited. ''I don't think I want to hear the worst part,'' I said at length. ''What is it?''

''John and Demos called the coordinator afterwards, to tell him of the shift in game plan, and it turns out he has written an identical personal letter to every Senator and Congressman on the Hill.''

I couldn't believe it. ''I can't believe it! Well, so much for rendering unto Caesar —''

John cut me off. ''It gets worse. Hatfield is now going to write his *own* personal letter to his colleagues in the House and Senate, advising them to have nothing to do with Washington For Jesus.''

''Well, I can't say as I blame him; I'd probably react the same way, in his shoes. But what a shame — the rally will be branded political now, no matter what we say, or how it turns out.''

"Yeah, probably," came the equally glum response.

"How is Bill Bright taking it?"

"Not good. As he said to John, he put his reputation and his whole ministry on the line, when he came on board. A lot of his evangelical friends had advised him against it — you know the sort of thing, 'linking up with emotional, irresponsible charismatics who were liable to shoot from the hip or go off half-cocked, *et cetera*'. . . . I suspect that from his point of view, right now their fears were well-founded.''

I couldn't think of anything more to say. "Well, what now?" I finally managed.

"I think we will probably get our own letter out to all the Senators and Congressmen, in which we'll do our best to assure them that, regardless of what they may have heard, our intentions are *not* political."

"I hope they read it."

"Me, too," John replied, and we said goodbye.

When I got off the phone, Dean was standing there, wanting to know what on earth had happened. I told him, adding, "You know, it's not too late for us to pull out of this. We haven't run any ads yet, or taken any orders. All we'd be out is our time, and a thousand dollars or so in travel expenses and phone calls.''

Instead of answering, he suggested we call John French, whose input he needed on a couple of the details. When they got done, I got on and told John what had happened. "John, I still feel that I'm supposed to do the book. But how can I write a treatment that uplifts Jesus and shows the body of Christ pulling together, if the whole thing turns into a political football?"

John's reply was as calm as mine wasn't: "You simply write a positive, uplifting, *honest* book. You tell it the way it is, and if it turns political, you tell that, too. The Holy Spirit will show you how to do it, without putting anyone down or embarrassing anyone. The trouble with you is, you *want* it to be non-political, and you're afraid it's not going to turn out the way you want it to. You're all wrapped up in what you want, instead of what God wants.''

John, too, was covenanted with Dean and me, to speak truth to one another, no matter how much it might hurt at the moment. It was a costly arrangement at times, like now, but it was worth it.

''Yeah, but —''

Dean frowned at me. He couldn't hear John's end of the conversation, but he had heard me say ''Yeah, but'' often enough in the past, to know that whatever was being said, I wasn't listening. I saw his expression, sighed, and started listening. And gradually I saw that that was all God wanted: an honest book.

For the first time in days, I had peace about the project. I wasn't happy about it, but I did have peace.

During the next few days, I did some checking by phone with friends around the country, whom I could count on to be honest, too. Most of those who had heard of Washington For Jesus were leery. They had already heard that it was political. One well-known southern pastor had initially considered coming, when it was just going to be a celebration. But when it looked like it was going to be more than that, and the rumors had begun that it was taking on a political cast, he decided to stay home. God was doing a new thing in his church, he said, and he felt his place was there with his people.

And then, a friend in Washington sent me the Washington *Post* piece that had come out on the Saturday following the press conference. I started to read it eagerly, for this article could well be the touchstone for the secular media. But the headline was brutal:

SUPPORT FOR CHRISTIAN RALLY HERE DRIFTING AWAY

And what followed was a classic job of editorial hitmanship. There was no doubt about it; Marjorie Hyer was a pro.

From my own experience as a trade editor in a major New York publishing house, I knew that it took only the selection of an adjective here, a slight omission there, and the cumulative reaction of the reader could be subtly redirected — in almost any direction the author chose. The New York *Times* prided itself on the most objective reporting in the business, but not even their journalists could go into a story entirely objective. A reporter was bound to have preconceived opinions and biases. And when someone was writing under a byline in one's field of expertise, one's opinions inevitably bubbled to the surface, and dictated the slant which the article took. Ms. Hyer's in the *Post* proved no exception:

> Washington For Jesus, a campaign to bring a million fundamentalist Christians to the nation's capital next month, has lost the support of some leading black clergymen here because of its right-wing political overtones.
>
> D.C. City Council member Jerry A. Moore Jr. (R-At Large), who is also pastor of the 19th Street Baptist Church, and the Rev. Dr. Robert Pruitt of Metropolitan AME Church have withdrawn as sponsors of the event.
>
> And an aide to D.C. Del. Walter Fauntroy, who is also a minister, said Fauntroy is "gathering more information" about the event and its sponsors to reevaluate support for it.
>
> Washington For Jesus has been billed by its promoters as an apolitical drive to gather more than a million Christians here on April 9 [sic] for a day of prayer and national repentance.
>
> But some of the campaign's promotional material — as well as its organizational structure — has raised questions about its real purpose.
>
> Nancy Brailsford, an aide to Moore, said he withdrew when he "discovered the campaign had some views" with which he disagreed, specifically when he "discovered they were anti-D.C. voting rights."
>
> She also said that Moore "has been in the forefront of the human rights issues, and this group [Washington For Jesus] is opposed to gay rights."
>
> Asked about the group's stance on D.C. voting rights, a spokesman at the campaign's Virginia Beach headquarters res-

ponded that "Washington For Jesus has no stand on political issues."

Asked about gay rights, the spokesman, who refused to give his name, replied that "homosexuality is an abomination in the eyes of the Lord."

Pruitt, who is listed on Washington For Jesus literature as a member of the "Washington D.C. Advisory Board," said that he never agreed to let his name be used that way. "Some young people came around and asked if I would sponsor a film on Jesus," he said. "That's all I agreed to."

The commercially distributed film "Jesus" has been bankrolled by one of the campaign's leaders and will be shown locally to promote the crusade.

The moving forces behind the rally are Bill Bright, head of Campus Crusade for Christ International, and Pat Robertson, who heads the Christian Broadcasting Network.

Both have worked to mobilize fundamentalist and evangelical Christians into a voting bloc that would make religious beliefs — namely conservative Christianity — a test of fitness for public office.

Robertson told a press conference here earlier this week that the crowds they hope to attract "are coming to support no candidate whatever for public office. We are coming to repent for our corporate sins. . . then to ask our fellow citizens to repent" of our sins as a nation, "then to call for a healing."

Some area religious leaders suspect, however, that the well-organized campaign has goals beyond prayer and repentance. Interchange, a loose coalition of religious, labor and public interest groups, has charged that "religious language is being used to mask a political agenda."

Most pastors of local mainline churches, as well as officials of the Council of Churches and the Interfaith Conference here, have spurned the prayer rally effort, because of such suspicions.

There was more in the same vein, and it would be read in editorial offices of major newspapers around the country and duly filed for the future reference of any other reporters that might later be assigned to cover WFJ. It was a tone-setter, and the tone that it set did not bode well for the future coverage that

WFJ would receive in the secular media, at least in the larger, more urbane metropolises, where there would be little or no first-hand contact with either local or national organizers, nor any desire for such contact.

It seemed instructive to examine the piece in detail, because it would be indicative of the sort of treatment WFJ could expect. My first reaction concerned the very first sentence, where she said that WFJ was losing the support of local black clergymen because of its right-wing political overtones. If the casual reader read no more than her lead sentence, that would be the impression he would go away with. A phone call to WFJ's Jerry Kantowski revealed that not one of the three black clergymen she named was ever approached to be on the steering committee, and there was no such thing as a "Washington D.C. Advisory Board," which she herself would have discovered, had she followed the basic rule of responsible journalism: *check your facts.* As for an erosion of black support, nothing was further from the truth, as she would have discovered had she checked with any of the black leaders who *were* on the steering committee — Bishops Winley, Patterson and Williams.

She did call WFJ headquarters to check out the allegation regarding the rally's position on D.C. voting rights, and whoever answered the phone told her that WFJ had no stand on political issues. Which only made sense: why on earth would a national rally ever inject itself into local politics? [I subsequently talked with most of the people working at WFJ headquarters, and only a few of them had the vaguest notion of what was involved in the issue. No matter, Ms. Hyer knew that her Washington readers would have a very clear understanding of the issue, and could be counted on to react negatively to the stand she attributed to WFJ.]

As for the question of homosexual rights legislation, the homosexuals had already begun clamoring that the rally was anti-homosexual, hoping to give the impression that all those people were coming to Washington for the sole purpose of protesting their rights. It was a tactic which they had used before to draw media attention to themselves, and apparently it had worked again. I did not blame whoever answered the phone for refusing to give his name: given the obvious hostility of the questions, I would not have given mine, either, especially when any statement of WFJ policy should rightly come from either the chairman of the steering committee, John Gimenez, the program co-chairmen Bill Bright and Pat Robertson, the director of communications, John Gilman, or national coordinator Ted Pantaleo. But not one of these five men was ever personally contacted by Ms. Hyer in the preparation of her article. And the way she phrased it, she made it look like whoever she did talk to was cowardly hiding behind his anonymity. Personally, I thought that whoever the unfortunate person was, he showed remarkable presence of mind by simply quoting God on the subject of homosexuality.

Something that bothered me more was the repeated use of unsubstantiated innuendo. "Some religious leaders suspect" — who were they? "Most pastors of mainline churches. . . have spurned the prayer rally effort" — who were these shadowy pastors? Then, as if to bolster the appearance of a case, she mentioned Interchange, referring to it as "a loose coalition of religious, labor and interest groups," which made it sound eminently respectable. She failed to mention that this coalition included the American Communist Party, the A.C.L.U., N.O.W., the pro-abortionists, the A.D.A., Common Cause and other left-wing groups.

By continually alluding to these suspicions of a hidden political agenda, it did not matter that she never corroborated them; eventually the reader was going to believe that where there was that much smoke, there was bound to be some fire. And admittedly, it *would* be hard for someone who did not know the Lord to believe that we were coming all that distance, simply because He had called us to. Once the possibility of supernatural motivation and purpose was removed, we would *have* to be coming for political purposes, no matter how staunchly we denied it.

The overall impression for the average secular reader would probably be that the rally was a loser to begin with — a bunch of Bible-toting hypocrites coming to impose their narrow, rigid beliefs on anyone they could get to listen to them, like the people you used to see in the park, or on street corners, standing on soap-boxes. Definitely something to be ignored and avoided. Which is, in the end, what the media did. There were two ways in which the media could do in a coming event: one was by finding scandal and exposing it; the other was by simply ignoring it, and thereby turning it into a non-event, something that might as well not have happened, for all that anyone heard about it. In some ways, the latter was even more effective than the former. In my years in publishing, I had seen a number of fine new books sink without a ripple, because no one had deigned them worthy of review space.

Angry and a little depressed, I put Ms. Hyer's article aside and called John Gimenez. If I had had any reservations about the project, I didn't have them any longer. "John? How soon can I get with you, to get started on gathering background material?

"Well! Welcome aboard, brother. We've got the leaders' meeting in Washington coming up next Saturday. Why don't you fly down and meet me in Charlotte Thursday night? Friday we'll pick up Bill Bright in D.C., and we both speak that night in Newport News, and then Saturday is the meeting."

"Good, count me in. And how about my coming back to Virginia Beach afterwards, to spend a few days there talking to people, and so on?"

"Sounds good," and he told me the name of the motel he would be staying at in Charlotte.

"I'll be there." And I was.

6

Ups and Downs

John Gimenez arrived in the motel lobby with two other men from his church. M.R. Welch owned the new twin-engined executive aircraft in which they'd flown down (as well as a construction equipment company large enough to support such a plane), and Austin Lindsey was a recently retired Naval Air Force captain, with thousands of hours logged in carrier-type aircraft. We visited for a while in the lobby and were picked up by Tim Kelton, pastor of the modest Four Square Church where John would be speaking that night.

John was in high spirits, as we drove through the night, and I marveled at his enthusiasm; whatever he would soon be sharing he must have said a thousand times before, during the past year and a half. Occasionally speaking in as many as three different towns in the same day, he had been going flat out without let-up almost since the beginning. If Washington For Jesus turned out to be a disappointment in terms of attendance, it would not be because its national chairman had not given his utmost. I shook my head; the man had to be under some kind of special anointing, to be able to survive that long on an average of five hours' sleep. And here he was, laughing and sharing anecdotes, as if this were his first week of evangelizing for the rally, instead of his eighty-second.

When we got to the church, perhaps 150 people were there — not even a full house. But if John noticed, it didn't register; he was undaunted. And the moment he started to preach, I became for the first time really glad to be doing this assignment. I had not fully realized just how key John was to what God intended to do in Washington on April 29th. Indeed, some people had said, why John Gimenez? But as he started to preach, I began to see the answer to that. To look at, he was not your Charlton Heston type, coming across as more "comfortable" than "commanding." But the moment he got into his message, you forgot about appearances. There was an anointing on him that was undeniable. One moment he would have you laughing, usually at some joke made at his own expense; the next, you might be wincing, as he pricked a sin that was a little close to home. Sin was a word that wasn't too fashionable these days. It was not a word that you heard in many big suburban churches, the ones with the manicured lawns and the shiny new sedans in the hedge-bordered parking lots. Sin and repentance were words that seemed out of place and out of time; they made people uncomfortable.

John didn't care. That night he told the people that God was calling His children to Washington to repent for their sins and to turn from their wicked ways, and they heard him. And many who had not been planning on going, or who had been on the fence, decided to go. He didn't tell them anything that he hadn't said countless times before, but it sounded fresh that night, and special, as if the Spirit had given it to him just for them.

I particularly liked the story he told to demonstrate how the rally was already cutting across old divisions and barriers in the Body of Christ. "I can tell you things you wouldn't believe!" he exclaimed. "I'm sure you know the in-fighting and out-fighting of groups like the United Pentecostal Convention and the Assemblies of God. No love lost, right? These (and he gestured to his left) are convinced that they (he gestured to his right) are going to hell. And I found out that *they* are convinced that *these* are going to hell.'' He had to pause there, to allow the laughter to subside. ''And so, Mr. Urshan was in town. He just happened to be the general superintendent of the UPC. He once played fullback for the Chicago Bears, and I was asked, do you want to meet him? I said sure. I went and shared the vision for Washington For Jesus, and tears came into that man's eyes, and he said that in the last ministers' convention of several thousand pastors, God gave him a word to preach on about reconciliation. He said it was time to reach out. There was a lot of misunderstanding, a lot of problems and division because of a lack of communication.''

John shook his head in mock amazement. ''I couldn't believe my ears! I had been taught that those folks were going this other way that I'm not going. And yet, as I looked in this man's eyes and heard his voice, I said, if this man doesn't know Jesus, he's awfully close to it!'' He stopped again for the laughter. ''He asked, would I come and speak to all their district superintendents? I said, sure. So I went out to St. Louis, and there were about fifty or sixty district superintendents from all over the country. I'll tell you, brother, I know the presence of the Lord, and He was there! They gave me an hour, and afterwards they came together around me, laid hands on me, loved me. And they voted unanimously: 'We'll do everything we can to support your rally.' You know,'' he said, breaking into a smile, ''that's got to be a miracle, because they thought all of you were going to hell.'' There was much laughter, which John joined, and then added, ''And I'm sure you thought the same about them!''

John held up his hand to still the laughter. ''God is trying to bring us together as one! See, we have got to understand that we can't just have a little revival here, a little revival there, a little fire over there. God wants to have a *big* fire! He wants the whole world to see His glory! 'And the glory of the Lord shall be revealed.' Jesus said, 'That they all may be one, that the world might believe that thou hast sent me.' There is no way — *no way* — that the world will ever know and believe that God sent Jesus until we get ourselves together! I'm not talking about union; I'm not talking about you and I having to see it exactly the same. We're one in Christ! The glory of the Lord *is* going to be revealed, and all flesh shall see it *together*. Why? For the mouth of the Lord hath spoken it!''

And in their hearts, everyone who heard him that night knew it.

Friday, March 28, dawned bleak and drizzly. John spoke again in the morning, and around noon we went out to the airport, to fly up to D.C., where we were to pick up Bill Bright at 3:00. Their pre-flight inspection completed, M.R. and Austin went up to the flight deck, while John and I stretched out in the cabin. Actually the cabin wasn't all that big — large enough for four reclining seats, two on either side of the aisle, facing fore and aft — but it was extremely comfortable. Just before take-off, our pilots each reached a hand back, and the four of us joined hands and committed the plane and the flight into God's hands. And with that, Austin eased the throttles of the Piper Chieftain forward, and we started to roll.

Our airspeed was about 230, when we entered the first bank of clouds. It got a little rough, and yet there was an uncanny sense of peace inside the plane. I could usually relax in a small plane, almost as easily as in an airliner. But this was different; it was as if we were small children, nestled in the hollow of God's hand. Almost immediately, John drifted off to sleep. And I drifted back to something he had said last night: if this *was* God's rally, then He was calling *all* His children who were able to come . . . and there was a terrible urgency in the call.

I had felt it in each discussion, each phone call — how important it was that we did respond to His call. Because the situation was even more critical than we had imagined, and we might not get too many more opportunities to even have such a rally.

It was not surprising, therefore, that those who had heard God calling them felt compelled to alert others — almost like watchmen trying to arouse a slumbering city. Hurry, hurry to the gates, to the battlements — we're under attack! We can only hold out a short while longer. But the city slept on. Who were those self-appointed watchmen anyway? We didn't pick them. If the enemy was in the vicinity, we could deal with him at dawn well enough. No need to get up in the middle of the night.

Disheartened, humiliated, these WFJ watchmen did not quit. They carried the word to the by-roads and the hedges, to the little churches and the four-corner towns. And there, plain folk did respond — people for whom it was difficult to arrange to get away from work during a non-vacation period, who could not easily afford the cost of going all the way to Washington in April, for whom it was not a lark, or a "fun thing to do for a change," or "a great experience for the kids." For them, it was more like a spiritual pilgrimage, undertaken in obedience to the beckoning of God, and they were content to trust in His miraculous intervention to make the trip possible. These were the people that John Gimenez preached to last night, that Pat Robertson was speaking to every day. And that was why John and Pat and the others were redoubling their efforts; because they were finally getting through.

John awoke as we entered the landing pattern for Washington's National Airport. We talked a bit about the increasing hostility of the press — Billy Graham was now being quoted as having come out against the rally, which John was sure was categorically untrue. And even the Christian media weren't getting the story straight. John told me that two magazines had reported he and Jerry Falwell were joining together to lead an anti-homosexual rally. The sad thing was that, regardless of any subsequent correction, tens of thousands of Christian readers had formed a very wrong opinion of the rally's purpose and might well have decided not only to skip it themselves, but warn their Christian friends to stay away from it. As for Jerry Falwell, Pat had approached him personally, and asked him to join with them, but he had replied that while he wholeheartedly supported the work that Pat and Bill Bright and the others were doing, he did not feel that he could join forces with any work of an ecumenical nature. Too bad, I thought, because if Washington For Jesus was any indication, it looked like the major works that God would now be doing in America would be of an ecumenical nature, bringing many parts of the Body of Christ together for His purposes.

I mentioned my thoughts about the press's attitude towards WFJ, in light of the piece in the *Post*. There was a strong temptation to succumb to a siege mentality regarding the media: in fact, one could become almost paranoid about the press. But that attitude was as dangerous as the incredible naivete of some Christians who believed that if they were totally open and honest, the secular press was going to respond in kind, treating them fairly and positively, as they would other people. The trouble was, Christians weren't like other people: they had a supernatural Savior, who had redeemed their lives and called them to selflessness, and who would help them in response to prayer. But remove the possibility of the supernatural, which a skeptic would do as a matter of course, and the only other explanation was that one was dealing with gullible folk who were hopelessly self-deluded and being led by hypocrites of the worst sort.

John nodded. "I've always been a fighter, you know. Where I grew up, we used to run up and down the streets shooting at each other. And we always knew that if we went into a certain area, there would be attacks. So we found out how to get around those areas, how to maneuver and not get trapped. And now I find the same thing: there are danger zones, and you've got to find out how to get through them. So, now I've learned something about these media people: the best thing to do is not to say anything. Because no matter what you say, they're going to twist it to make it sound like what they want it to be, or what they suspect." He sighed. "So — you don't have to tell them everything you've got in your head. I'm finding out that, unless you're talking with spiritual people, the less said, the better off you are. Because the world can't understand. And yet we give them credit, time and time again, that *maybe* they'll understand. How *can* they? When the carnal mind absolutely and completely does not understand the things of God?"

I nodded, and we both fell silent, looking out the window at the clouds as we began our descent. Say as little as necessary, I thought, and let your actions speak for themselves. To say more than was necessary was foolishness or an ego-trip, and we weren't called to be foolish. We were called to be wise. Harmless — but wise.

"Incidentally," John said, "we've decided to do away with the declaration entirely. We never could get the wording right, and I finally said, do we really need a declaration? Isn't II Chronicles 7:14 all the declaration we need? They agreed, and so we're going in the spirit of II Chronicles 7:14, and that's all."

"That's enough," I agreed. "You couldn't sum it up any better than that, anyway."

The rain let up, as we lined up on the runway and settled steadily lower, until trees and buildings were rushing by outside. You could almost feel the main wheels reaching for the ground. Then they touched, and the nosewheel joined them, and soon we were taxiing up in front of the executive air terminal, to park alongside other craft, some of which were so sleek they made ours look almost common. After we made our way inside, M.R. and Austin went to file a flight plan for Norfolk, and John and I waited for Bill Bright. I asked John just how Bill had come to be involved, as that had to be one of the major miracles God had done in preparation for WFJ.

John had first met Bill at the dedication of CBN's new facility and had briefly told him about Washington For Jesus. The next contact had been made by John Gilman, on December 12, when he had spent more than an hour with the busy head of Campus Crusade for Christ. John Gilman explained that while the concept had begun with the charismatics, they felt that God intended for it to be enlarged, that He wanted the whole Body of Christ represented there on April 29th. And because of some things that had been happening recently in Bill Bright's own life, he was completely open to the proposal and would consider joining Washington For Jesus, even though it could mean losing friends and support if he did so. He would even consider canceling his own plans to organize 25,000 pastors to meet together and pray and intercede for the nation in late November of 1980, in favor of the earlier, April 29th, gathering. That was how urgent he felt America's situation was.

Needless to say, it was not long before a follow-up meeting was arranged, at which John and Anne Gimenez, Demos Shakarian and Jack Cohen of Greyhound spent almost four hours with Bill Bright, at the end of which he made his commitment. "You know what he told me?" John asked. "He said, 'I'm willing to put my ministry on the line, because I believe this is of God.' Another thing: he was going to have a meeting of his international directors at the same time — hotels, meeting places, all the arrangements had already been made. You know what he's doing? He's canceled that meeting and is bringing them all to Washington!"

"Whew," I exhaled. "It makes you stop and think, when some of our own charismatic leaders tell you they have 'schedule conflicts,' or too much happening at home."

"Yeah," John replied, "and let me tell you something else: you know how the press has been accusing him of being politically motivated? Well, practically every time we talk, he reminds me, 'Now, John, we have to make sure that this is not, and does not get, political. In no way can we let it; I've given my friends my word, and they trust me.' The press is accusing him of wanting to make it political, and all the while he's the one who's fighting the hardest to make sure it's not!''

Inside the attractive general aviation terminal, we made a few phone calls, and then settled into the blue upholstered chairs to await Bill Bright, who was not long in coming. He arrived, wearing the dark blue suit that was his trademark, and with him was his sandy-haired aide, John Jones, a bright and well-organized former newspaperman who always looked like he was in a hurry. We got back on board the small plane and took off for Norfolk, where John and Bill Bright would meet with Pat Robertson. The meeting was going to take place right at the airport, because John and Bill were scheduled to speak to a meeting of pastors and leaders in Newport News that same evening, and would be flying out as soon as the meeting was over.

We prayed again before take-off, this time with six hands joining. And once again there was that uncanny sense of peace as we lifted off into the gathering dusk. This flight was subdued. John and Bill chatted a bit, but mostly we looked out the windows and kept our thoughts to ourselves.

It was raining again when we landed in Norfolk. The airport manager had made his own office available for this meeting of WFJ's steering committee chairman and the two co-chairmen of the program committee. I was privileged to sit in, and noted the efficiency with which headquarters coordinator Jerry Kantowski and his assistant Carol Owen presented the budget as it then stood: a staggering $186,000 was needed within the next six days! There had been no formal fund-raising campaign, and although contributions were nonetheless coming in from all over the country, they wouldn't begin to cover their immediate requirements.

Yet the three chairmen did not seem to be interested in the budget — or the rest of the meeting's crowded agenda. Instead, they spent their time fellowshipping with one another and bringing each other up to date on what was happening. Bill, for instance, had just heard from Billy Graham, who was so incensed at having been misquoted about the rally, that he had written them a letter, which they were free to make use of, stating that Billy Graham was 100% behind their non-political rally, and wished he could be there himself. And the only reason he wouldn't be there was a long-standing commitment to Indianapolis, where he and his team would be staging a city-wide crusade the same week.

To see them so exuberant, and to see how close they had grown since being yoked together on this project, was oddly reassuring, on a level I barely understood. But I still couldn't help wondering if they were going to accomplish all that needed to get done in the hour they had left. And glancing over at Carol Owen, I could see her stealing a look at her watch. Finally, they did get around to discussing facts and figures: $85,000 for the speakers' platform, $50,000 for the rental of the sound equipment, $47,000 for the portable toilets —

"*$47,000?*" Pat exclaimed.

"Well," Jerry replied calmly, "we've got to have them, and this is the firm that can deliver all the ones we're going to need."

On each general item, there was some discussion, and occasionally they got bogged down a bit in minutiae. Something struck me about half-way through the meeting: John Gimenez was doing very little of the discussing, content to leave it to Pat and Bill. Was he over-awed by them? After all, each of these men headed ministries whose operating expenses were around a million dollars a week. No, it suddenly dawned on me that that was not it at all. John was a humble man. In his place, I could imagine myself just waiting for an opportunity to make a contribution and justify my being a part of it. But John's ego did not work that way. When he spoke, it was almost with reluctance, but what he had to say cut to the core of the problem and frequently provided the necessary course correction.

I also noted that Bill, too, seemed to be cognizant of John's input. I had no idea what kind of appraisal was going on in his mind, but Bill was a careful man, not given to rash judgments where people or projects were concerned. Indeed, his very stability was one of the reasons why he had such rapport with top businessmen around the country.

As for Pat — well, Pat was Pat. As on television, he was always totally honest and upfront about how he felt about things, never hesitating to go right to the heart of the matter, often with a twinkle in his eye. Ever since I had been the editor on his book nine years before, I had known him to be a perseverer; once he'd made up his mind about a thing, he would see it through, no matter what. He was not one to suffer fools gracefully, or those who pushed themselves on him, and yet I had a hunch that he admired John for the perseverance which had brought him back to Pat's office a third time, after two polite rebuffs. Pat was 100% behind the rally now, and would remain so for the duration. Three perseverers — all in all, quite a combination.

There were ten minutes left before we had to go out to the plane, or Bill and John would be late for their meeting in Newport News. And still nothing had been settled about where this huge sum was going to come from, if Washington For Jesus was going to remain operational. I looked over at Carol, who bore a permanent expression of polite desperation, and even the unflappable Jerry Kantowski was beginning to look the tiniest bit flapped. And then, almost as an afterthought, Pat made a second large commitment from his organization, matching a second one that Bill had recently

made, and John committed all of his remaining reserves. The
monetary crisis was abated — for the moment. And there were
even a few minutes left for some bantering fellowship as the
meeting broke up.

Outside, the night mist glistened on the tarmac as we
approached the silhouette of the plane. Once more we joined
hands for prayer, and taxied to the end of the runway. The
engines whined up to max power, we started to roll, and lifted
smoothly up into the night sky. Again, it was mostly quiet on
board; each of us was lost in thought. But not for long — the
next field was only twenty-five miles away. Scarcely had we
climbed above the cloud cover than we were descending again.

On the ground, we were driven over to a high school auditorium, where a sizable crowd of pastors and lay leaders had
already assembled. John opened the meeting by reminding
them of the verse in Genesis 49: "Not unto John Gimenez. Not
unto the Baptist Church. Not unto the Lutheran Church. Not
unto any other group. But unto *Him* shall the gathering of the
people be! And that's exactly what God is doing. He's
gathering His people from every corner of this nation, to give a
demonstration that He is still Lord of the universe. He is still
God. He is still Sovereign. And no matter what man says, no
matter what man may legislate, in the end it's going to come
out exactly as He planned it to come out."

He told them how the vision for the rally had come to him as
he was preaching about David and Goliath. When he got to the
point where David said to his brother, Did you not hear what
the King said? *Is there not a cause?* it was then that God began to
say the same thing to him. Was there not a cause in our nation
today? And then he said, "The one thing that God wants more
than anything else, I feel, is to see this fragmented, divided,
divisive Church of His come together in one place and in one
accord, that He might demonstrate His glory to His people."
But there was something else that we were coming there to do,
and that was repent. "We, the Church, must repent. We're

always trying to get the sinners to repent; *we* need to repent. God says, 'If *my* people' — not the devil's people, or the unregenerate, but *my* people, who are called by my name. He's putting the demand on the Church. And if we want the healing of this nation to occur, we can't say Mr. Carter, repent, or Senators of the United States repent, or Congressmen repent. He said, '*my* people,' and that, brothers and sisters, is you and me!''

John then introduced Bill Bright, in terms so ringing that the latter was a trifle embarrassed. "John," he said, chuckling, "that introduction reminds me of a man who was introduced as a great statesman, a great scholar, a great orator, and a great man — and he believed it. As a matter of fact, he could hardly wait to hear what he was going to say. What's more, he wouldn't speak to anyone for days afterwards, so impressed was he with his greatness. Finally, he broke the spell by asking his wife, 'I wonder how many really great men there are in the world?' She said, 'I don't know, but there's one less than you think.' ''

He waited for the laughter to quiet and then continued in a serious vein. "Bill Bright is not great. But he worships a great Saviour, to whom he became a slave twenty-nine years ago. He has been my Master and my Lord, and I gladly acknowledge Him as my Master, from my first awakening moments, until I lose consciousness in sleep each night. He is the first person I talk to every day. He is the last person I talk to every day. All day long, I walk and talk with Him, and I love Him with all my heart.''

It was an unusual opening, yet I was glad that he had opened just that way. The audience was almost wholly charismatic, I guessed, and while Bill might never have spoken in tongues, he was clearly as led by the Spirit and surrendered to the Lord as any person in that auditorium. Well, I thought, it was as if someone had said: if our eyes were truly on Christ, and our hearts yielded to Him, it really didn't matter what doctrinal

background we came from. We could work together and
fellowship together, and the quality of our faith would be
evident in the fruit of our work.

He reminded them of what God had said to Moses in
Deuteronomy, chapter 8: "God said, 'When you've eaten your
fill, bless the Lord your God for the good land He's given you.
For that is the time to be careful. Beware that in your plenty,
you do not forget the Lord your God and begin to disobey
Him. For when you become full and prosperous, and have fine
homes to live in, and when your flocks and herds have become
very large, and your silver and gold is multiplied, that's the
time to watch out that you do not forget the Lord your God
who brought you out of slavery.' And so, our nation, born out
of the slavery of Europe, as our founding fathers came out of
bondage to perfect a new nation — our nation has become the
most prosperous in the world. . . . And now we have turned
from God. And we've disobeyed God. We are worshipping
idols. . . . The chastening of God, the judgment of God is on
America, because of the Christians' lukewarmness, carnality,
disobedience. God judges a nation because of His people. He
doesn't judge a nation because of its non-believers."

He then went on to share his insight regarding the plagues
visited upon this nation following the Supreme Court decision
banning prayer in schools. And this time, as I heard it, I found
myself thinking, well — maybe. God *had* entrusted this land
into the hands of the Christians. I had seen that clearly and
unequivocally during the research for *The Light and the Glory*.
And our schools were one of the key places in which we had
trained our sons and daughters up in the way that we would
have them go. For three centuries American schools had been
perfectly comfortable with God's presence, even grateful for it.
And now, suddenly in the span of a few years, we had gotten so
lukewarm, and the idealists' influence so pervasive that
suddenly atheists' rights had become the dominant issue.
(Today the issue was homosexual rights, and who knew what

tomorrow would bring? Rapists' rights?) That decision, which denied the presence of God in the schools of the republic which He had created and protected, just could have been the thing that finally brought God's patience with His people to an end. *His* people, because it was we Christians who had let it happen. And not just in the schools, but everywhere, all across the board.

Bill went on. He was concerned that night about the shocking military jeopardy this nation was in — and that most of the nation didn't seem to be aware of it, or believe it. "One Congressman told me last night in Washington, as I was in his home — and he's a member of a committee that is briefed regularly by our military men — that every time he gets briefed, it takes him days to get over the shock. He said, 'Would you believe that the Soviets could take us over in three days?' You say that we have enough nuclear power to destroy the whole world ourselves, and therefore the Soviet Union is not going to attack us, because we would destroy them. But what most Americans do not realize is that, in violation of the SALT agreements, the Soviet Union has developed a highly successful civil defense program. . . . We have no civil defense program. They also have a highly-developed anti-ballistic missile program. We have none."

Bill did not use figures that night, but I had heard them on the news the week before. Because of their ABM and CD systems, in the event of all-out nuclear war, Russia would lose 20 million of its 243 million. We would lose 160 million of our 220 million. I could remember the stunned realization which came over me as I thought about these figures: in the wake of Afghanistan, the hitherto unthinkable was now something we had better start thinking about.

Bill was not shouting; he was speaking quietly and dispassionately, as he expressed a deep-felt concern for our ability to defend ourselves. And yet, because he dared to express that concern out loud, because he dared to think realistically about what the idealists had chosen to regard as simply unthinkable, he was pilloried in the press. Apparently, in some circles it was a crime to suggest that America might be inviting a major conflict by refusing to consider its possibility.

Another thing our Early American research had revealed was that God did indeed seem to be on the side of the Continentals, favoring their cause with more than one sudden fog or snowstorm to mask the movements of Washington's troops, and incidentally receiving the credit in countless diaries, journals and letters written by the soldiers of the day. Ironically, the one time the weather turned savagely against the Yankees was when Congress had sent Benedict Arnold north to annex Canada. Their meteorological and coincidental "luck" turned totally against them — only to turn back again the moment the retreating remnants of their band were back on American soil. It seemed that while God did not look kindly on military adventures for the purpose of acquiring territory, He did intend us to defend that territory which He had given us, and which had hitherto been preserved at such a cost in toil and shed blood. What was the Scripture which had swung so many devout Christians into the active defense of the embryonic republic? Galatians 5:1 — "For freedom, Christ has set us free; stand fast, therefore, and do not submit again to a yoke of slavery."

If we were going to stand fast today, we had no choice but to take a realistic world view, as well as being realistic where individuals were concerned. The idealist maintained that man was basically good — because he wanted so badly to believe that it was so. The realist knew that, as Scripture said, man was a fallen creature, and there was no good thing in him, save Christ, and Him crucified. Well, the same was true of the world. "Human rights" was a high-sounding but empty phrase where a Christless society was concerned. The Brotherhood of Man had never existed without the Fatherhood of God, and never would. And our idealists could not will a Christless society into fraternal behavior simply by wishing that they would want to behave in a beneficent way. It was rampant foolishness, and a great many of us Christians had also been guilty of that kind of wishful thinking. And so, as with so many other things, what had happened over the past thirty years to our ability to defend ourselves was *our* fault, not the idealists'. They were acting in accordance with their faith. We weren't.

In the meantime, our present posture seemed about as logical as Alice's Wonderland: the further into the sand that we plunged our heads, the more likely we were to get our tail-feathers chomped. And yet the mere suggestion that we take our heads out of the sand and look around was enough to spur some idealists to cry "Hawk!" and label the suggester as being slightly to the right of Darth Vader.

By the time the meeting was over, and we were once again on board the plane and joining our hands in prayer, it was after ten. One more leg of our journey and then to bed. We were flying back up to Washington to spend the night, before the major leaders' rally there the following morning. As Austin called the tower for our take-off instructions, I reflected that I had never been up and down in an airplane so many times in one day before. Charlotte to Washington to Norfolk to Newport News to Washington — if I had ever had a fear of small planes I would either have been cured by now, or be a basket case. As it was, I hardly noticed it, and thinking about it now, as we passed through 2,000 feet, I could almost sense a huge unseen hand holding the plane in its palm.

7

Unity or Disunity?

That night, as we flew the final leg of our journey, up to Washington, no one was tired or preoccupied. The meeting had gone well, and there was every reason to suspect that the big one tomorrow at George Washington University's auditorium would go as well or even better. Bill Bright was more relaxed than at any time I'd seen him. He felt like talking, and I had my hand-held recorder, and so I started asking questions. Earlier in the evening, he had mentioned that repentance was the key; what did he think would happen if we failed to repent?

"I think if we do not repent, we will not only continue to experience the plagues I referred to tonight, they will grow in intensity and number, until we are literally destroyed as a nation. Morally and spiritually, to say nothing of economically, we'll become bankrupt. I think we'll lose our freedom as a nation, either through direct military takeover, or blackmail by the Soviet Union, or through subversion. In any case, we'll lose our freedom. . . . And it could happen within this decade, possibly in the next two or three years."

Earlier, when he had been speaking on the importance of our taking responsibility for where America was spiritually and morally today, for some reason I had thought of Germany, in the late twenties and early thirties, before Nazism had really gained an iron grip on the country.   There were a few ministers, like Bonhoeffer and others, who had tried to awaken Christians to what was happening, but they were unable to do so.   Did he see any parallels there?

"Yes, I see a great parallel to what happened in Germany, and what also happened in Russia.   Because the Russian Orthodox Church held sway in the lives of tens of millions of Soviets.   In both countries, the Church was in existence, but not active.   Their people were mostly historical Christians, but not personal Christians.   By that, they didn't know Jesus Christ in a personal way.   They were playing games with God, just as we're playing games with God in America.   But I am optimistic to believe that whereas the Soviet Christians did not awaken, and the German Christians did not awaken, we *are* awakening.   Personally, I believe we're going to see our land healed.   I believe we're going to see a great spiritual awakening.   I believe we're going to see a dramatic change in the media and in government and education.   I believe God is going to do something incredibly great in our nation.   But first there must be a revival.   And revival follows repentance."

Since Bill felt like talking, I took the opportunity to ask him if he would care to tell about how he had come to know Jesus Christ in a personal way.

"I was a businessman.   I'd been an agnostic through high school and college.   I was on the faculty at the Oklahoma State University extension, and then went into business in California.   In the process, I met a group of Christians whom I admired and respected.   Until then, I had never met a successful businessman or professional man who was a Christian; I'd just assumed men were supposed to be strong and self-reliant.   Women were supposed to be the spiritual ones, as in my mother's case. . . . So, as a matter of intellectual integrity, I was forced to consider the life of Jesus.   In the process, I received Christ.   I was not immediately changed, but was gradually changed so dramatically that I spent the next five years at Princeton and Fuller Theological Seminary, where I ran my business on the side. I never planned to be a minister, but I wanted to know everything I could about Christ and the Bible."

He smiled at the recollection. "Of course, the more I learned about Him, the more excited I became. And so it was in 1951, in a very dramatic way, God gave me a vision that embraced the whole world and impressed upon me that He wanted me to help fulfill the Great Commission — to carry the Gospel to the ends of the earth." He looked over and smiled. "Well, you've got to start someplace. So the ministry began on one campus. God led us to start at UCLA, and the first year there was a tremendous impact for Christ on the entire campus; the whole atmosphere of the campus changed."

He remembered something and backtracked a bit: "Prior to that, I'd made a very important commitment which I think is relevant. My wife and I had been married for three years, when we made a decision. At the time, we were both very materialistic and very ambitious, and we liked the good life, the luxurious life. But the Lord showed me that I could only wear one suit of clothes at a time. I could only eat one meal at a time, and I couldn't take anything with me when I died. All my dreams of fortune — which were becoming a reality, because I worked hard day and night to make money — were not important. My priority was to seek first the Kingdom of God. . . ."

His voice trailed away, as he seemed to be remembering that moment. Then he continued. "So, one Sunday afternoon, we got on our knees in our home in the Hollywood hills, and we signed a contract, literally relinquishing all of our rights to God, and we became slaves. The Apostle Paul says in Romans 1:1: 'I am a slave of Jesus Christ.' That day I became a slave of Jesus Christ, and I determined that I would live for Him alone, whatever it cost, for the rest of my life, and my wife did the same." He looked out the window at the night sky. "It was a couple of weeks later that God gave me the vision for this worldwide ministry. But I'm sure that He never would have entrusted me with that vision, had I not first made that commitment."

Up forward, Austin was talking to the tower at Washington Airport, and we would soon be on the ground. It had been a very long day for all of us. And a very good one.

Saturday, March 22nd — the sky was overcast, as we drove over to George Washington University's auditorium. As always, there was no way of telling how many people were going to come. The auditorium held 1500. . . . when we got there, the Youth With a Mission people had already set up tables in the lobby, and were putting information out on them. I remembered what a tremendous help the YWAMers had been at Boston's "Great Awakening" two years before, and I was glad to see them here in Washington, pitching in, as there was no way that the WFJ staff, stretched as thin as it was, could possibly have done it alone. Ron Boehme, who would be emceeing the meeting, came up and told me that Nick Savoca, YWAM's New England director, was here. Glad to see Nick again, I went over to chat, and before we knew it, it was almost ten.

I took a seat in the first row, in order to use my camera, but I could have sat practically anywhere, because there couldn't have been more than three hundred people present. I knew that numbers were not supposed to matter, that "God brought those whom He intended to be there," and so on, but I couldn't help wishing that there were more. If a million people *were* going to come to the rally, someone had figured that three hundred thousand would have to come from the D.C. metro area. That being the case, this meeting, for the local pastors and lay leaders, should have been packed out, instead of filled to only 20% of capacity. . . .

The meeting was about to begin. We opened by singing "All Hail the Power of Jesus' Name," and now John Gimenez addressed himself directly to the people of Washington: "We don't come to Washington with clenched fists; we come with open hands. We don't come with curses on our lips, but with praises for the Jehovah God. We don't come demanding something for selfish reasons, but we come demanding something so that this nation can once again return to the reality of goodness and honesty and decency." He lowered his voice and spoke in a confidential tone: "I think you all know we're in trouble. Unless God does something on behalf of this nation, we're all going down together — no difference between black, white, Puerto Rican, tall, short, rich, poor — it's going to affect everybody."

And then he came to the message of the hour. "You know, the greatest weapon that the Enemy has used against the Church is the spirit of division. . . . he is trying to keep us away from each other. This has been his tactic for many, many years. Look at us here: all backgrounds, all denominations, yet loving the same Lord, Jesus Christ. We agree! But let us get on to these other little areas, and we start fighting, and it's been the Enemy that has brought the breech, that has vexed the churches. Even now, you'll find many forces trying to misinterpret, trying to keep us separate. But they won't succeed come April 29th. You know who'll be there? Those of us who have heard the sound, who have heard the voice of the King, who said, 'Gather unto me.' We're going to be there, and we're going to have the largest prayer meeting ever held in the name of the Lord."

As John went on, something occurred to me: one of the things the Enemy feared most was the spectre of the Church at last coming together in spirit. For Satan knew what it said in the Book of Revelation. He, too, knew the signs of the end times, and that the unity of the Body of Christ heralded the end of his reign on earth. For centuries, playing on the base-nature self-righteousness and jealousy of spiritual men, he had kept the Church divided, and he was doing it still. "Who is this John Gimenez? I've never heard of him; probably another would-be visionary on a trip." Or, "I can't understand Bill Bright associating himself with a bunch of charismatics. Everyone knows they're of the devil. But, then, I've been wondering a lot about him lately." Or, "Well, everyone knows Pat's father was a Senator. It's only a matter of time before he comes out of the closet himself politically. I mean, this year a movie actor. . ."

And then I heard something else in what John was saying: if the rally was of the flesh, it would fail, as it deserved to. But if it *was* ordained of God, then any Christian who heard about it and who didn't at least pray with an open heart to see if God was calling him or her to go, was in disobedience. And what I heard John saying was, if they were operating out of a spirit of *dis*unity, they could not possibly hear God telling them to go. The opposite was also true. As John put it: "Those who are hearing from God are moving in the spirit of unity. And those who are not hearing from God are moving in the spirit of disunity." And it seemed more true today than at any time in the past.

The next speaker was Jesse Winley, of whom I had heard John speak more warmly than of anyone outside of his immediate family or staff. This small, old, unpretentious black man strode to the lectern, looked out at the audience with a baleful eye, and waited for silence.

I waited with anticipation. John had said that it was Bishop Winley who had repeatedly encouraged him, when he was really down, and who single-handedly had inspired 10,000 people from the New York City area to commit to coming to the rally, which meant that his influence carried well beyond his Soul Saving Stations. As he waited, barely able to keep from pacing, I had the thought that here was a grizzled warrior, a lion in the winter of his life, supremely confident of the Holy Spirit, who was about to put the words on his tongue.

When he finally spoke, it was with great deliberation, slow and measured; he was not the least concerned about drawing it out too far. The audience sat transfixed, sensing that they were watching a volcano about to erupt. They were right.

"I have been deeply burdened about our unpreparedness," he began, enunciating each syllable ominously. "You see, our churches have not been citadels or fortresses. They have been entertainment centers and social clubs with limited member-ship. Here we find ourselves facing the Enemy, and we really don't know how to handle it or what to do. Therefore, we find in ourselves a lot of divisions, a lot of criticism, persecuting each other, and I'm quite sure that the Enemy has done this. My prayer is that God will so anoint our eyes that we will *see* what God sees. . . ."

There was more in this vein, as the bishop warmed to his subject, and predicted an explosion of holiness. And then, seemingly out of nowhere, he gave us a picture that cut right to the heart of the matter. "Right where our church is, about a half a block away, the hit men came through the block during a drug war, and blew a guy's car up, with the guy in it. I looked out the front door, and there across the street were all the gays, hugging and kissing and everything, right in the middle of the street. And down at the corner, there was a bar. This girl had gone out to work for her pimp. She had made a bundle of money, and she'd blown most of it. And while she was trying to explain to him what had happened to it, he took out a razor and just slit her throat. She fell to the floor and was dying. And while she was bleeding to death, some men stood over her. They were betting two to one that she wouldn't live."

The hall was stunned, and the bishop waited until we had recoiled — and assimilated the horror he had described. Then: "And the Sunday after that, God the Father spoke to me, and do you know what God said? Three things: there is more grace in Harlem than there is sin. He said, there is more grace in New York City than there is sin. There is more grace in the *world* than there is sin. For where sin abounds, grace is much more abounding! And God said, 'Get your eyes off sin and get your eyes on the Son, *and preach Jesus! And His grace! Let us go forth in Jesus' name, despite immorality —* ' '' The rest of his words were drowned out in a tumult of enthusiasm, as we rose to our feet applauding and cheering.

But the bishop wasn't finished. And as he waited for us to sit down, it occurred to me that he had just brought us up to date: this was how much worse the inner city had gotten in the twenty years since *The Cross and the Switchblade* was published. It was also clear that the bishop was a combat officer. This was no rear-echelon general with a comfortable house and swimming pool and chauffered cars. This man had come straight from the trenches, and would be going back there, as soon as this meeting was over.

The bishop told one more story before he quit: "I want to tell you about divine love, and unity," he said, in a voice barely above a whisper. "I want to tell you about something that happened to me just recently. My teachers and I and a couple of ministers were invited to a conference by a very distinguished educator. We were the first to register, and they had some beautiful new cabins right on the water. But they wouldn't give us those cabins; they had some other, older ones way back out there somewhere, back in Texas — I mean, a real bad place: even white folks was scared to go out there." There was a burst of laughter.

"They gave the new ones to a group of other preachers, and these were of a part of the country that was known to have heavy feelings. Here we were, way back in these woods, and I was ready to take it in low key, because I wanted to get back home —" There was a pause, and then everyone laughed. "So I said, 'Brothers, let's not — let's stay here in these cab-

ins. They're old, but they're all right; we can sleep in these —''
They said, 'No, we want to go to the new ones!' Now, two of
the fellows I had with me were northerners. . . .'' He slowly
shook his head, and everyone laughed.

"So they overruled me and grabbed their bags, and they
started walking toward the new cabins. And we met in there
with about eighteen white preachers, from Mississippi, Alabama, Louisiana, Georgia, Florida, Arkansas, Missouri,
South Carolina and North Carolina. When the three black
preachers and all those white preachers met in there — you talk
about blessed quietness, holy quietness!'' There was a roar of
laughter, and he raised his hands, continuing in a whisper:
"Listen to me: that thing was so thick in there, you could feel
the demons of Hell!''

"You go ahead and tell it!'' a black woman called out, and
everyone chuckled.

"Now, Lord, here we are!'' the bishop shouted. *"The
Christians!* The ones who are entrusted with the way! There we
were, stalking each other. So, my friend from the north, he
took his briefcase and put it up on one of the bunks, and started
quoting Scripture, about how good and pleasant it is for
brothers to dwell together in unity. I said, 'Brother, *shut up!*
There's no unity here! You'll end up being lynched, and you
talk about unity?' '' We laughed, grateful for a moment's
release from tension, and he again raised his hand and lowered
his voice: "Listen: that was one of the worst things that I have
ever felt.'' There was absolute silence in the auditorium.

Bishop Winley continued in a more normal tone. "So, Dr.
Howard heard about what had happened, and he sent for me
and my group and put us in the new cabins. And all night
long, I couldn't sleep. The Spirit of God visited me all night
long — crying, weeping, ministering in the Spirit.

"And early the next morning, God said, 'Get up!' And I got
up and started walking across the lawn. And then here was one
of the other brothers, and when we were meeting each other,

we had our arms out, like that," and he held his arms wide to embrace the other man.

"He said to me, 'Brother, all night long God was talking to me.' And he said, 'I'm sorry about what happened last night.' And I said, 'I'm sorry,' and we cried together right there, and we prayed.

"He said, 'Let's go and have coffee,' and the next thing you know, they all started gathering around. And then, all of us were together, and we started sharing together and talking about the things of God. And then after that, we started giving testimonies and telling where we were from, so I gave my testimony of what the Lord was doing in Harlem. They wanted more, so I told some more, and they wanted still more. Then someone said, 'Tell you what we'll do: we're going to cancel this next session and just let the bishop come and share with us.' And they did.

"That night, the place was packed. It was jammed, and it was God's opportunity! You talk about divine love — God anointed me to preach that night as I have never preached before. And everybody in there was crying, *melting!* And that night, we had unity, like some of us had never known before. . . ."

The bishop went on a little longer, but I knew I would never forget the story that he told, and I sensed that there were quite a few people in tears at the telling. When he finished, I was surprised to find that I had gone through an entire tape, recording him. He had preached for better than an hour, but I was so absorbed, I wished he could have gone on all morning.

Pastor John Meares of Evangel Temple in Washington stood up next. White-maned and lean, in an elegant three-piece suit, he had the poise of a southern aristocrat as he graciously welcomed the out-of-towners and graciously took an offering. And then Bill Bright spoke. Jesse Winley was a difficult speaker to follow, but Bill did not change his delivery. He spoke simply and directly, and the people listened respectfully at first, and then enthusiastically.

The last speaker of the meeting was a complete surprise: Abraham Lincoln. Actually, it was an actor named Fritz Klein, doing his impersonation of Lincoln, from a monologue which he had compiled from all of Lincoln's speeches and addresses. My initial skepticism was soon replaced by appreciation for the tremendous amount of work that had gone into getting the smallest gesture right, down to polishing the rimless glasses which perched half-way down his nose. For the next quarter of an hour, he *was* Lincoln.

"Friends, Omnipotence condescended to take on Himself the form of sinful man, and as such, to die an ignominious death for their sakes! It behooves us then, to humble ourselves before the offended power. And in sorrowful remembrance of our own faults and crimes as a nation and as individuals, let us pray that the God of our fathers may not forsake us now!" As he made this plea, in the background the words and music of the Battle Hymn of the Republic softly and gradually swelled until they filled the auditorium and our hearts, and old Abe folded his speech and with stooped shoulders left the stage.

For the second time that morning, I found my eyes filling with tears.

Tuesday, April 29th, 5:30 A.M.

"And the deaf shall hear"

8

Never So Few

That night, comfortably settled in the Rock Church's guest house next door to the church property, I slept more soundly than I had in days. Sunday morning dawned unusually balmy, and faced with an hour and half before the morning service, I pulled on my running shoes and went out to explore some of the housing developments in that tidal flat area. Heading for the shopping area at the corner, I figured if I took a right turn every mile or so, I would wind up approximately back where I started from.

I figured wrong. I wound up so far back in the boonies that it took some prayer and a lot of left turns before I found my way back to the church. I made it to the service on time, but not half an hour early, as I had been advised to do, if I wanted a good seat down front. Happily, there weren't any bad seats in that extraordinary church, though when I got there, it looked like every one of the three thousand seats was taken. But some people obligingly scrunched over and I settled on the center aisle at the back. The uncanny feeling of proximity to the platform area, which I had sensed on my first visit, was even more noticeable with the church filled and people up front. And not just people, but a robed choir and a full-dress band.

The service was an upbeat, fast-paced, freewheeling affair,

alternating between the well-trained choir singing original modern anthems, and John Gimenez preaching in his unique manner, to which I found that I had now become accustomed. He "wore well" — he was easy to listen to, and he usually had a slightly different approach to his subject than had occurred to me before.   Throughout the remainder of the service, periodically there would be a chorus or two of Bible verses set to music, and several people shared informally, all of which was greeted with enthusiasm.   In fact, enthusiasm was the watchword that morning.

That afternoon, everyone more or less collapsed, and that evening there was another service, similar to the morning service, except that the preacher this evening was Anne Gimenez. Anne was an ordained minister in the Assemblies of God, and she had been a traveling evangelist for four years when she first met John, soon after he had become a Christian and was himself traveling with "The Addicts," an acting troupe of ex-junkies like himself.

Like her husband, Anne preached with fire and feeling, unafraid to stick her neck out, or call sin by its rightful name. Nor was there any sense of jealousy or competition on her part; she was the perfect support to her husband. All in all, they made quite a team, and the people of Rock Church loved them. In fact, John would not accept the salary that they wanted him to have, so they put it into a "Pastor's Discretionary Fund." It was this money that John had committed to Washington For Jesus, at the recent co-chairmen meeting at the Norfolk airport.

The following morning, I walked over to the end of the education wing of the church, which had been given over to Washington For Jesus — and got the biggest surprise since beginning the project. I don't know exactly what I expected — large rooms filled with people answering telephones, huge wall maps, people typing, others bustling here and there on very important business — but the reality could not have been further from it. Aside from Ted Pantaleo's, there were no private offices, and Ted's was all of nine feet by twelve. In fact, there were only five other people working at Washington For Jesus that morning: Jerry Kantowski, in charge of the WFJ headquarters; Cush Dobbs, a carpenter and general trouble- shooter who was responsible for the putting up of the speakers' platform and sound towers; Jim Cucuzza, whose job it was to set up all communications, both here and on the Mall; one of the volunteers who was manning the phones; and John Gimenez's sister Ann, who was handling incoming calls and acting as receptionist. That was the sum total, and the rally was four weeks away!

"I can't believe it!" I exclaimed to Ted, after he had shown me around (which took about five minutes). "Here you are, with maybe a million people about to descend on the Mall, and you have fewer full-time people on your staff than groups planning conferences less than a twentieth that size!"

"Well," he explained, "you know how short we are on funds. And those conferences — they usually have registration fees, don't they?" I nodded. "Not only have we been stymied in figuring out how we could register everybody, we have de- cided against taking any sort of offering on the Mall."

Again I nodded; I could see the wisdom in that, given the attitude of the local press. Still, it was a shame, because if everyone who came chipped in a couple of bucks, that would cover all the expenses. And yet, I could just imagine the head- line:

Christian Rally Takes in a Million Dollars in One Scoop

"So you really are utterly dependent on free-will contribu- tions?"

"That's right," Ted replied, "and it seems to be the way God wants it, for now anyway. But that's why we have only three paid staffers. I'll tell you something, though," he said, leaning back in his chair, "some of our volunteers are worth more than we could possibly pay them, even if we had the funds to do so.''

I agreed. I had already seen the work that Carol Owen and Sharon Wise, the layout designer, were doing; and Bart Pierce, the associate pastor who was in charge of the youth rally at RFK stadium the night before; and John Gilman, who was so busy he was nearly running into himself coming around the corner.

"Somehow," Ted sighed, "it all gets done. Don't ask me how, but it does. And except for the perpetual shortage of funds, which simply means that we can't do all the things we'd hoped to do, we're even fairly well caught up."

And they were. Volumes of mail were going out, and state by state the rally was actually much better organized than at first glance it appeared to be. In each of the fifty states, there were the four designated coordinators: a youth coordinator, a women's coordinator, a spiritual coordinator (he was the one responsible for collecting the intercessory prayer lists), and an overall coordinator who was responsible for everything. In addition, there were seven regional coordinators, who were to oversee the handling of any problems in their areas of the country. These various coordinators were also charged with arranging accommodations and transportation, and pre-rally rallies in their respective states, to raise the interest-level and spread the word. That, right now, was the biggest job of all, because it seemed like, despite the fact that a number of mailings had gone out nationally and regionally to every church in the country, the majority of the Body of Christ still had not heard more than the vaguest of mentions, if that. In Arizona, for instance, four mailings had been sent out to churches in the past two months, and still people were saying, "What's Washington For Jesus? How come we haven't heard about it?"

Now, in the final weeks before the rally, state coordinators were going directly to the media with the story, and often, sad

to say, finding the secular media more responsive to news of
the rally than the Christian media. In all their endeavors, WFJ
headquarters provided any assistance that it could, sending
literature, and sometimes speakers, too, where possible. Even
John Gimenez was able to squeeze one or two more
engagements into his already impossible schedule. On the
whole, the system was working remarkably well. My friend
John French, the administrative assistant for Arizona, told me
that his state's contact person at WFJ, a volunteer named Dr.
Don Seim, had repeatedly been helpful far beyond the call of
duty, and they had developed a close bond of fellowship over
the phone, without ever having met.

The secret, of course (other than the grace of God), was anticipation. Jim Cucuzza, for instance, had already worked out
with the phone company the sort of lines that he would need
into the two recreational vehicles which would function as the
transportation center and the on-site command post. Francis
Owen, Carol's husband, who was in charge of transportation,
had sent parking instructions to the more than five hundred
buses which had already pre-registered. Bart Pierce was in
constant contact with the officials at RFK stadium, as well as
with the entertainers, who would be donating their time and
talent for free. Jerry Kantowski had lined up enough sound
equipment to ensure that the speakers would be heard from 7th
Street to 14th Street, even though he had had to cut back on the
original quantity of speakers, because of lack of funds. John
Gilman had edited and laid out the WFJ newspaper which
would double as a program, listing such pertinent information
as the location of parking, first aid stations, lost and found, and
portable facilities.

But it was really not until Tuesday morning that I came to
fully appreciate how well prepared the staff was. At ten
o'clock, Jerry and some of the others were scheduled to meet
with the "Mayor's Task Force" — 34 top representatives from
every concerned department in Metro D.C., from the Metro-

politan Police to the Transit Authority to the National Park
Service to the Fire Department, even to the Secret Service.
This group of hard-nosed professionals met regularly to formu-
late their own plans regarding rallies such as WFJ's, or the
anti-nuke demonstration that was scheduled to take place the
weekend before Tuesday, the 29th. That one was supposed to
be attended by Jane Fonda and Tom Hayden, and they were
saying that they were going to bring 200,000 protesters with
them — as many as had come for the famous anti-war rally of
1967, which was the largest crowd ever to assemble on the Mall
for one event (not counting the '76 Bi-centennial celebrations
during the week of the Fourth of July).

I asked if I could go with them, when they met with the
Mayor's Task Force, and they said fine. I was picked up at
about 5:30 AM, and on the way to the airport, Jerry and Carol
filled me in on their initial dealings with the task force. At first
they could not have been more skeptical. Captain Mazur, the
head of the Metropolitan Police, had asked Bart Pierce point
blank: "Who in the world told you to bring 55,000 young
people to RFK stadium in the first place?"

"Well," Bart stammered, "we all feel that God has told us
to be there."

Whereupon the Secret Service agent reached across and
punched the captain in the arm and said, "Looks like you've
been outranked there, Captain!" and the whole meeting had a
good laugh.

One of the first questions that they asked was: "Are you a
First Amendment group?"

"What's that?" was Jerry's reply, and they explained that it
was a protest group, which invariably came stridently demanding its rights as granted under the First Amendment, to hold
free assembly. What was more, the police and park service
people were paid public servants and were obligated by law to
do this, that and the other for them, and so on.

"When we learned that," Jerry said, "it helped to explain

the near-hostility with which they initially greeted us. But we had come in exactly the opposite attitude. We said, 'Look, you're the experts. We need your help. Tell us what we should do, and we'll do it. We'll do everything in our power to cooperate with you, any way that we can.' "

Now Cush spoke up. "Apparently, that was so unusual that their attitude towards us began to change. When they saw that we really meant what we said, and that we were coming in humility and not arrogance, it got to the point where they couldn't do enough for us."

"You'll see when we get there," said Jerry.

Traveling up to Washington with us was a broad-shouldered young man with dark, curly hair and a battered trenchcoat. This was John Crossley, a taxidermist who, while touring in eastern Europe, had learned a technique for making glass eyes for stuffed animals that was so good his product was sought by taxidermists and natural history museums all over the free world. Yet, in a sense, his business was little more than a sideline which financed his main concern: working behind the Iron Curtain in Rumania, where he had been instrumental in saving the lives of a number of Christians in prison there.

He told me about one — a man named Gheorghe Calciu, who was a spiritual Orthodox priest whom he had met last year. Father Calciu had already been in prison for sixteen years, the last three in an underground cell, where he had seen no light for three years. When John met him in Bucharest, Father Calciu knew that he was about to be re-arrested. He stood up and kissed John on both cheeks and said, "You know, meeting a brother like you, and you telling me that people care about someone like me, makes what I've suffered worth while." Father Calciu was re-arrested that same week and was tortured for four days and four nights, and John got out of the country by the skin of his teeth and hasn't been allowed back in since. "He told me something else during that meeting we had," John recalled. "He said that every day that he spent in solitary confinement, he prayed for America, for its leaders, and that we would not lose the freedom that they had lost. You know why they arrested him? He taught that Christ, and not the secret police, was the head of his body. That kind of teaching carries with it a sentence of ten years, but it might as well be life, because the conditions are almost unendurable. At this moment he is in the prison of Aiud, near the town of Sebes in the Transylvanian mountains."

In the course of our conversation, it came out that he had been down to Virginia Beach to see about the possibility of saying a few words at the rally, on behalf of fellow Christians in Rumanian prisons. "You have no idea what the public mention of a few names can do, or even just showing their faces on posters that are picked up by TV cameras and broadcast around the world by satellite. The slightest bit of publicity is often enough to free these men and get them exiled."

"Really?" I replied, a little skeptical. "I would have thought it would have the opposite effect, getting them even worse treatment for being trouble-makers, and bringing embarrassment to the government."

John nodded. "Normally it might. But Romania enjoys 'Most Favored Nation' status where America's foreign trade is concerned, which allows them to have World Bank credits and import and export bank tariffs, and things like that. Their balance of trade is precarious as it is; if they were to lose that Most Favored Nation status, they could not survive in the world marketplace. And they could lose it, if it were proven that they were in gross violation of international human rights clauses."

He shrugged. "We could prove that right now; in fact, there has already been one investigation by the House Ways and Means subcommittee just last year. Unfortunately, there were three security agents from the Romanian Embassy in the back of the hearing room, and the Romanian witnesses were so intimidated by their presence that they refused to speak. The

Congressmen didn't understand what they could be so afraid of and even mocked them, saying, 'Would you like a policeman to hold your hand?' But they wouldn't talk, because they had family back in Romania, whose lives they would be jeopardizing by doing so.''

Having written the story of the Basansky family's escape from the Ukraine, I knew how deep the control by fear went, and what John told me did not surprise me. At the same time, it would be unfathomable to any American without firsthand knowledge of it. "So, at the moment," John concluded, ''by publicizing the names of certain religious prisoners, we can sometimes get them released and deported.''

"What happens to them then?''

John laughed. "Why, if they need a sponsor in America, they can have a job in a certain glass eye factory in Ottsville, Pennsylvania. I've got five of them there already, with another on the way. Before long, we'll have a bit of Transylvania in Pennsylvania!''

Suddenly I got an idea: "If I were to mention the names of some of these prisoners in the book, would that help?''

"Of course.''

"Then go ahead.''

"Well, I've already told you about Gheorghe Calciu. Another man in much need of help would be Gheorghe Brasoveanu, a strong Christian who was one of the men who started the free trade union of Romanian workers. This was a trade union which called for the rights of workers, the rights of people in Romania to receive compensation for their labors and not to have to work in dangerous conditions or suffer on their jobs. He wrote a beautiful charter — a classic human rights document — and the moment it was broadcast in March of '79, he was arrested. Originally, he was put in a psychiatric hospital and given forced injections of drugs, but after pressure from the West about psychiatric abuse, he's been transferred to another prison, I believe to Aiud.''

He looked at me, his head cocked. "Have you got room for any more?"

"Sure," I said. "I wish we could give the whole book over to you."

"Well, here are two more: the first is a born-again Adventist in a very bad situation. His name is Murcia Dragomir, and he was arrested because he refused to work on the Sabbath day. He took a stand for that, and has been severely beaten many, many times. Finally, there is Costace Ababei, the son of Lydia Ababei, of the town of Iasi, in Romania. His mother was put in a psychiatric hospital, because she started a prayer meeting for Israel, the government's logic being that anyone who would pray for the Jews had to be mentally ill. We put pressure on the Romanian Government through Radio Free Europe broadcasts, and she was released. Her son, Costace, however, was drafted into the army, at which time they accused him of stealing weapons. He was beaten so badly that his mother didn't recognize him. If he was convicted, he could get the death sentence."

There wasn't much I could say, except that I would see that that information got published. He was grateful for that, and out of curiosity, I asked what was taking him to Washington. Was it more to do with imprisoned Christians?

"Yes, but not in Romania. In Cuba."

"In Cuba?"

He nodded. "Two young American missionaries — Tom White from Los Angeles and Mel Baily from Norfolk. They were flying over Cuba, dropping Gospel tracts, when their plane crashed. It happened about a year ago. They were tried and given four years for violating Cuban air space and twenty years for distributing anti-revolutionary propaganda."

I exhaled. "That's a long time to spend in a Cuban prison. What do you think you can do?"

"I don't know, but we've got to do something."

We lapsed into silence then, and I gazed out the window at

the bright morning sun shining down on the clouds beneath us — so white, so clean, it was hard to think of wretched souls being tortured and beaten, and praying to God in darkened cells. But then I recalled Solzhenitsyn's mind-searing epic, *The Gulag Archipelago,* that burst upon Western consciousness six years ago. No one who read that book could remain indifferent to the plight of fifty million souls in Communist prisons. I wondered how many forgotten Murcias and Gheorghes were praying for America right now.

After saying goodbye to John Crossley, we took the subway to RFK stadium, arriving at the meeting just in time. Representing Washington For Jesus were Carol and Francis Owen, Cush Dobbs and Jerry Kantowski. Representing the Mayor's Task Force were some thirty-four men and women, some in uniform, sitting on both sides of a long table. Their attitude was relaxed and sympathetic, even cordial, as they each asked questions pertinent to their particular department.

Once again, I saw that anticipation was the secret to WFJ's readiness. When asked for the latest figure on the number of registered buses, Francis Owen was able to report that in excess of a thousand buses were coming for sure, which meant more than 40,000 people right there, and that number would probably double within the four weeks remaining. The thought of that many buses suddenly converging on Washington with their tanks nearly empty was ominous, so Francis had advised them to refuel well outside the city limits. Also, for those which decided to come at the last minute and therefore could not receive the registration packet, WFJ information booths would be set up on all the major arteries leading into the city. Anticipation was the name of the game.

"You say that you're going to have Pat Boone and other

high-profile entertainment types coming — what sort of security arrangements have you made?''

Jerry answered that one. ''We have contracted with a private security agency to provide plainclothes agents to guard all of our key people and guests for the duration of the rally and the pre-rally events, like the youth rally and the women's and pastors' meetings. Also, this agency will be responsible for the security of the speakers' enclosure.''

The decisions went on — yes, there could be a TV camera up in the top of the Washington Monument; no, the Jumpers for Jesus could not do a sky-diving routine, landing in the Mall — and on. And gradually I came to have a better understanding of just how immense an operation this was going to be. The entire Mall was going to be literally curb-to-curb people!

The meeting finally broke up, and we went back to the center of town and had lunch at one of the inexpensive but attractive restaurants that clustered within walking distance of the Congressional buildings. They seemed to be favored by young aides who wanted a change from the cafeteria fare but did not have a whole lot of time or money.

I had some questions: First, what about the task force? I was amazed at their attitude; it looked and sounded like they were going out of their way to be helpful.

''For months,'' Carol Owen said, ''when we would talk about several hundred thousand people coming, maybe even a million, they just laughed and looked at one another and shrugged their shoulders. 'We have demonstrations all the time in this city,' they said. We found out later that the rule of thumb that they use is 10% — whatever figure the sponsors of a rally or protest or demonstration tell them is coming, they take a tenth of that, and that's the size of the crowd that they prepare for. But we never gave them inflated figures — if we didn't know, we said so, and we always told them only how many we were certain were coming. And then, all of a sudden,

in our January meeting with them, everything changed! I
don't know what did it; we had really prayed that the Lord
would just turn the meeting, and we came well prepared, and
our presentation was good. Anyway, the Lord just gave us
favor, and after that they started taking us seriously and
couldn't do enough for us.''

How did they get Metro to run subway trains in the small
hours of the morning?

"Well, we had to do something," Cush explained. "We
couldn't have thirty or forty thousand young people walking
through a residential area of the city at two or three in the
morning, on their way to the Mall. Even if they were quiet,
people would be so alarmed at the size of such a crowd moving
through the night that they would be jamming the police
station's switchboard. The best thing would be to move them
underground, so we tried to figure out how we might use the
subway. And there was no way. The subway closes at midnight, it had never been done, and the unions would never let it
happen. There was no way they were going to open before
six.''

Jerry picked up the story at that point. "But we kept trying,
and then we went to this task force meeting, and Bart Pierce
was there. Now a subway ticket for that distance costs 50¢, but
Bart pushed the wrong button on his pocket calculator,
working out what it would cost to buy 40,000 tickets in
advance, and got it in his mind that it would be only $2,000.
So he said, 'Look, supposing we bought 40,000 tickets up
front, would that make a difference?' Well, it did. You could
see that on their faces right away. And the man from Metro
nodded and said that he would have to check, of course, with
his superiors. . . .

"You realize," Jerry laughed, "that this was the first I'd
ever heard of this proposal. So as soon as we got out of there, I
said to Bart, 'Hey, man, where are you going to come up with
the twenty thousand?' '*Twenty* thousand?' he said, 'what are

you talking about?' I said, 'You'd better check your addition again.' And the look of stunned chagrin that came over his face would have been funny, had he not been in such pain."

"But you know," Carol said, "God used that. The next thing we knew, Metro made this public announcement of the unprecedented decision to operate twenty trains at three in the morning, for Washington For Jesus. And if it hadn't been for Bart's mistake, it never would have happened."

"Now all we have to do is figure out where the money is going to come from," Jerry added wryly.

They had been saying a great deal about the high places, but what about the valleys? Weren't there ever times when they had felt like they'd simply had it?

Jerry was quick to concur. "Yeah, that time came for me just a few weeks ago. One day I was just fed up with the blunders and everything that was going on, and I walked away from the office and headed towards home, saying, 'I quit. That's it; I don't want anything further to do with it. I've had it.' And as I walked, the Spirit witnessed to me. God seemed to be saying to me: 'I don't need you. I could bring someone in today, anyone, to take your place. I could put all the figures that you've got in your head, into his head. It is a privilege that I have called you to serve in that position.' "

Jerry looked down at his plate. "My heart melted. My attitude completely changed, and I said, 'God, forgive me. Let me be a part of this.' And I turned around and went back to the office and got back to work." He looked up. "So the whole thing boils down to attitude. This rally is not our thing; it's God's thing, and He's going to see to it that it's done in the right attitude, with the right motives."

Was that pretty much true for the others?

"Sure. A lot of my people that work for me — they come in, and they're really upset, and they're right, in the things they think; they're justified. Only they're totally wrong, because they've come in the wrong attitude. When they change their attitude, then God blesses it, and it's a whole different thing. What we need is a *servant attitude*. I can be a railing Pentecostal, casting demons out of rocks and dancing all over the place, and if I also have a real servant attitude, I can come up to a funda- mentalist Baptist, and I can serve him, esteeming him higher than myself, and God will see to it that we can come together.''

That said it about as well as it could be said, I thought, as we left to go over to Constitution Hall, to make final arrangements for the women's and pastors' meetings on the 28th. If the rest of the key people connected with the planning had attitudes like Jerry's and his friends', one could not ask for better spiritual groundwork. Maybe the rally was going to turn out to be God's, after all.

9

Go West,
Middle-Aged Man

When we finished at Constitution Hall, admiring the magnificently-renovated auditorium that would seat 3600, and which was available for about a quarter of the rent I would have imagined, we went out to the airport to catch our flight back to Norfolk. I had a few minutes, while we waited, to talk to Anne Gimenez and get some idea of the sort of woman it took to free her husband up enough to spend so much time on the road. As it turned out, it took someone who was willing to pay a rather steep price.

Anne was at that '78 camp meeting in California when John first shared his vision for a national rally, and she didn't take it too seriously: "Oh well, hallelujah, here we go again!" But then, as he started moving out on the new assignment God had given him, and his trips became longer and more numerous, she had a real problem with it. Because he was, in effect, leaving her to provide the leadership of a church of some 4,000 members.

And then one day, she was listening to someone else preach, and while it was a message she already knew the truth of, it was something she needed to hear. It was about Joseph, who had to recognize that it was not his brothers who had put him in the position he was in, it was God. "The Lord spoke to me then," said Anne quietly. "He said, *You feel that your hands are full, and you are blaming John. But can you not see that John has not put you in the position you are now in; I have?*" Her heart changed dramatically after that. She was thankful for what time they did have together as a family, when John was home, and she did her best to make sure that he was not burdened with unnecessary problems.

She did not usually travel with John, but one time she did was when they and Demos Shakarian and Jack Cohen called on Bill Bright. When it came time to pray, they prayed in a circle, each taking a turn, and as Anne waited, she thought, "They've already prayed everything I can think of to pray." But when her turn came, the words came to her: "Lord, we know who our enemies are; now help us to know who our brethren are. Help us to come to know them." And He did. Throughout their travels, they discovered that they had brethren they never dreamed of, people they might have even once considered enemies. And she saw so clearly that there was no time left anymore to harbor grudges or indulge in division, no time left to build kingdoms or reputations or great ministries. All that could be done now was get together and do God's will as fast as we could. Otherwise, there would not be enough civilization left to enjoy a big name ministry.

That evening, riding home in Jerry Kantowski's truck, I asked him about Sister Anne, as they called her. He told me of a recent experience in the headquarters office. "We were praying for Washington For Jesus during our morning prayer time and Sister Anne happened to come in. She joined our circle and started praying and she said very strongly: 'The Lord has shown me right now that the enemy is attacking us in two areas: *discouragement* and *division*. We're going to find that a lot of people are going to drop out. They're going to weigh the cost, and they're going to say, "I can't, I don't have the time, I can't deliver the goods, it's too much for me." But that's all right, because God wants us to weigh the cost. But we *have* weighed the cost, and we're willing to pay the cost.' And that was a true statement. We are willing to pay the cost."

On Wednesday I went over to CBN to see Tim Francis, assistant to chief engineer Sam Tolbert. Tim readily gave the credit for the incomparable technology in their new studios to his boss, commenting that technicians from NBC had told them that NBC did not have as up-to-date an installation as CBN. He also told me how moved he himself was by the remarkable spirit of cooperation amongst the three Christian networks, as well as the independent channels, like Jerry Rose's 38 in Chicago, and 24, and some personal ministries with equipment. That kind of interfacing was important at the top level, Tim said, but it had better be happening down where tech met tech. And it was.

He was talking about camera placement, and the miracle of being allowed to have a camera up in the Washington Monument, when it suddenly occurred to me: what would they do with all those expensive cameras out in the open if it started to rain?

"It still goes on. We don't have another day. In the meetings, everyone had said, 'If it rains, it rains. If it doesn't, it doesn't.' It won't rain; I'm convinced of that. Take CBN's dedication: it had rained solidly for two days before, and the ground was sopping wet. I said, 'Well, we'll probably have to cancel or postpone.' That's how sure my faith was. Turned out, we had a beautiful, beautiful day for the dedication. God has favor on His people."

That evening, after the Rock Church service, John Gimenez, John Gilman and John Jones from Bill Bright's staff got together, with Jerry, Carol and myself in the background. The purpose of the meeting was to hammer out the order of speakers, first for the pastors' meeting on the eve of the rally, and then for the twelve hours on the Mall itself. They figured they would be all done by 11:30. At midnight, the schedule for the pastors' meeting was barely completed, and the main day hardly begun.

I had often wondered how such schedules were arrived at. I knew now: painfully. I never dreamed how much consideration went into placement, balance, pace, and timing, to say nothing of bruised egos.

"We can't have all the black preachers so close together. . ."

"But if we give him a slot in the 10:00 to noon 'prime time,' we've got to do the same for him and him, too. . . ."

"Do you realize we've got 48 minutes of programing here without a song?"

By 2:00 AM, my own worksheet had been scratched out and re-written so many times that it looked like something on the bottom of a birdcage. We were surviving on peanutbutter-cracker sandwiches and warm soda filched from the church's school pantry, and everyone was a little punchy. By 3:00, we had to cudgel our concentration to keep it focused, and practically had to stand on our heads to keep our eyes open, but the agenda was taking shape. No speaker was allotted more than ten minutes, and most of the speakers, even people like Pat Boone, David DuPlessis, and Demos Shakarian, would have no more than eight. Eight minutes — most of the preachers I knew couldn't get warmed up in eight minutes, let alone wrapped up. It would be a real test of self-discipline and obedience, especially when they would be speaking before the largest live audience that any of them would ever address.

The last name went in the last time slot at 4:00 AM, and we stumbled to bed. I was too tired to sleep and could not shut my mind down. I was flying home the next afternoon for Easter, and then Monday was going out to Arizona and California.

John Gimenez had felt very strongly that if I possibly could, I should talk in person to key people like Jack Cohen, Demos, Jack Hayford, Jim Coffaro and Violet Kiteley, rather than try to do it over the phone. "Also, you need to find out for yourself whether the West Coast feels as strongly about Washington For Jesus as we do here. For us it's a four-hour drive; for a lot of people out there, it's a four-*day* drive, if they come. You'll want to find out if they're coming."

What he was saying, in effect, was, in the immortal words of Horace Greeley, "Go West, young man;" only at the moment I felt every one of my forty-three years. Oh well, at least didn't have to go by stagecoach.

"Those of you next to windows should have a good view of Big Muddy, as she passes underneath," our pilot announced, and though I had an aisle seat, I was still able to get a glimpse of the Mississippi. In a moment it was gone, and I thought how easy it was to forget what a big country America really was. What with television and instant news, and stagecoaches that traveled thirty thousand feet up in the air at nearly the speed of sound, one entered into another dimension of reality from an age when it might take the better part of a summer to get from sea to shining sea.

But it was still possible to get a feeling for the sheer immensity of the continent by driving across it, which was almost a luxury in today's terms, where every hour counted. My partner Dean and I had driven to Denver in '78, for the Christian Booksellers' annual convention, and I treasured the memory of that trip with those of taking the sleeper from Cleveland to New York when I was a boy. In the car, Dean and I usually bit off a little more mileage than we could chew, but every so often we would squander an hour, get off the Interstate, and mosey through little towns like the ones we grew up in, with shade trees and "Main Streets" and white clapboard churches. They were so much alike, it was uncanny — not in a ticky-tacky way, but because Americans, when you scratched them deep enough, were surprisingly alike — in the way they thought, in the way they lived, and in the way they built their towns. And despite what modern idealists a couple of generations removed from them might think, there were still an awful lot of them who cared about God, and about living their lives for Him. And now people were moving back to the small towns, in search of the wholesomeness and neighborliness they vaguely remembered there, often not realizing that these things originally came from the well-spring of the townspeople's Christian faith.

I leaned back and closed my eyes and recalled, like color slides, favorite scenes from that trip — the lush, green hills of Tennessee right after a rain shower. . . the town in Missouri that was having a street fair, complete with parade and fire engines. . . the corn of Kansas, higher than the car, mile after mile after mile. . . and then the wheat fields of the Great Plains, shimmering golden red, under a fat copper sun just at sunset, with the red-gold haze rising to meet the red sky, and the silhouette of a lone grain elevator standing out on the horizon. *America, America, God shed His grace on thee. . . .*

I was met at the plane in Phoenix by John French, with whom I would be staying for the next four days — four extremely busy days, judging from the agenda he had worked out for me, which even included breakfast meetings which, I gathered, were growing in popularity among busy execives who didn't have enough lunches available during the week, to get everything done. At the top of the agenda was a Washington For Jesus rally that evening at a local church, and I had just time to shower and change.

For a state which had been slow in getting started, Arizona had certainly built up momentum in a very short time. Two buses would be leaving from Phoenix, departing at 1:30 AM

Saturday morning, and getting in to Harrisonburg, Virginia, at 2:30 Monday afternoon. As much as I loved driving across America, I thought, I was not sure how much I would love sixty-one straight-through hours of it, even if I could leave the driving to Greyhound. And speaking of Greyhound, I was introduced to Jack Cohen, the executive vice-president, who was on the steering committee and had been one of the men to call on Bill Bright. While he was quick to downplay his role or any contribution he might have made, John told me confidentially that a word from him had made available Greyhound's vast, highly-computerized group travel department, which had the facilities to coordinate the logistics and accommodations of practically everyone traveling to Washington for the rally. I told John that I would really appreciate a chance to talk to Jack at length sometime, and he replied, "I anticipated that, and I already have you down for dinner with him and his wife Marge on Thursday."

I was touched by the amount of loving care that had obviously gone into the decorations for the banquet — red, white and blue bunting everywhere, red and white carnations on each of the tables, and at the end of the hall, behind the speakers' lectern, someone had put up some very realistic silhouettes of people with their hands raised towards a huge sign that spelled out Washington For Jesus. There may not be all that many people going from Arizona, I thought, but each one who was going really *cares*. Indeed, as I looked around the tables, enthusiasm was the watchword — there were a hundred and thirty people there, and they were like a bunch of kids about to embark on a school field trip or church picnic.

Also there, was Jim Coffaro, the West Coast regional coordinator, down from Oakland for the occasion. It was good to meet him, even though I was going up to San Francisco in a few days, in part to talk to him. When it came his turn to speak, I noted one thing he said, by way of warning, to those who had decided to come: "It is unbelievable how the enemy has tried to deter this particular mission. I was flying here in a plane recently with my brother and the pilot, and we ran out of gas. It was three in the morning, in the middle of a blinding thunderstorm, but God brought us down, when there was practically no way! God is in this thing. And the enemy is at work. . . . You are going to have every conceivable obstacle put in your way. If you're in business, things are going to happen in the days to come that will make you say, 'It's impossible for me to get away.' Now as for me and my house — in my place of business I will have a sign that will say *Closed, Gone to Washington For Jesus.*''

Thursday morning, I had a chance to talk to Marge Eckman who was in charge of transportation and had enough enthusiasm for the entire state! And she enjoyed her work — in fact, she was having such a ball helping people to work out their travel plans, that she was considering opening a small travel agency after the rally was over. One of the things that excited her the most was the continual awareness of God's hand on her endeavors; it was almost as if the Lord were standing beside her desk, as she was on the phone.

''One of the first couples who contacted me said, 'Pray with us that we can sell our camper, because that's the only way we can afford the trip.' I did, and their camper sold. Another time, a gal named Lou called at nine in the morning and said, 'Have you got room for one more?' And it so happened that I did, because two other gals had just canceled out, leaving one room. 'How much is it?' I told her: $261. 'Well, would you agree with me that I will go? Because I really feel that the Lord wants me to.' I did, and she called back two hours later, all laughing and happy; someone who owed her some money had apparently just repaid their debt. Lou could go!''

She beamed, her tight blond curls bouncing on her head. ''I got a call from some ladies in a town called Ajo, which is south of here, about forty miles from the Mexican border. They wanted to raise money to send other people who couldn't afford to go themselves, and they asked what it would cost. They'd already collected a hundred dollars. They had decided to have a sale of Mexican food, and they asked me to agree with them in prayer that it would be a success. So I did. Well, they went to the butcher, and told him what they wanted meat for, and he gave them $35 worth. They went to the city officials and asked if they could rent a hall to have the sale in, and they gave them the use of the hall for free. And so it went — at this point they have raised enough money to pay the way for two people and still have a hundred dollars for a third person. And they couldn't be more excited!''

Was she going with them on one of the buses? No, but she had gone to Washington on a similar bus trip a couple of years earlier, and the way she described the spirit and the fellowship, it sounded very much like the modern-day equivalent of a pilgrimage, but in the old-fashioned sense of the word: a responding to a call of God which brought them forth on the road together, sharing not only a common goal and worship at their destination, but Christian companionship along the way. Apparently, not that much had really changed in the six centuries since Chaucer saluted April as the month in which ''folke longe to go on pilgrimages.''

I had a good talk that noon with Arizona's state coordinator, Derald McDaniel, who told me that one of the first things he did was move to indefinitely postpone an Arizona rally for Jesus, scheduled for May. ''Everywhere we turned on that one, we kept running into a blank wall. And we found that our attention was divided. . . . What we determined the Lord was telling us was to concentrate entirely on the Washington rally. So we've completely dropped the Arizona rally for now.''

Would he care to comment on the motivation of some of the people from his state who were going? ''If ever there was a Joel trumpet call, it's got to be this one. One of the men in our Wednesday pastors' luncheon said that the cost of division is too high under the present circumstances. If world conditions were not what they were, we might be able to afford the luxury of disunity. But it's just too high a price to pay now. . . . As C.W. Ward used to say, the ground is level at the foot of the Cross." He paused. "That's the call. That's the reason we're going."

I thanked him, and a little while later I got a call from Jack Cohen. Greyhound's national headquarters was in Phoenix and I was very much hoping to see their group travel division in operation. I had already imagined whirring computers and a large wall map with tiny flashing lights on it, but I was in for a disappointment. Apparently, because of the role Greyhound was playing in supplying transportation and arranging accommodations, the militant homosexuals had decided that the company was aiding and abetting anti-homosexuals, having never gotten it out of their minds that several hundred thousand Christians might be coming to Washington for some reason other than to protest their drive for new legislation. As part of their harassment of Greyhound, they threatened to picket several of the corporation's most visible terminals.

The vice-president of public relations handled their threat with commendable composure, stating that Greyhound was not anti-anything, and that if they cared to travel somewhere as a group, Greyhound would be happy to arrange accommodations for them and transport them anywhere. But the upshot of it was that the corporation became a bit gunshy where I was concerned, and asked that I not come over at all. I told Jack I understood and never mind, and looked forward to seeing him and Marge at dinner with John and Barry.

Jack was a fascinating character, an extremely successful businessman who had recently become a completed Jew. In fact, so new was he to the whole evangelical Christian scene that at first he was a bit awestruck by it all. God used his innocence to good effect, as it turned out. At the crucial meeting with Bill Bright, there was some discussion about the problems that evangelicals would have in working with pentecostals, and Jack, not knowing what a pentecostal was, asked Bill to explain it to him. Jack had never realized that in Christendom there were so many different persuasions, and he had said, "You know, I always thought that if you were Christians, you walked hand in hand down the same side of the street. I never realized there was such a division among Christians."

It was then that he suggested that, in the interest of unity, Bill co-chair the program committee with Pat, and that the national steering committee be made up equally of evangelicals and charismatics. As he told of this, I was again impressed with how it didn't really matter how many years a person had labored in the Lord's field, or how much wisdom he had accumulated thereby. All that mattered was a heart that was open, and a will that was yielded.

Another time when Jack was in a meeting with Bill Bright, his business acumen came in very handy indeed. It was an emergency call from David Schoch, David Kiteley and Jim Jim Coffaro: West Coast contingents had arranged with World Airways for a series of charter flights, but then World Airways had been closed by a strike, and when they re-opened, their Los Angeles sales representative was no longer with them and had apparently never made any record of his commitments. In the meantime, World had reassigned the allocated planes elsewhere. They said that they might be able to get them back, but it would have to be at a price that was double the amount originally agreed upon.

"They were desperate," Jack recalled, "so I said, 'Look: there's no sense in everybody worrying. That isn't going to solve the problem. Leave it to me; *I'll* worry.' So I called World Airways and got the executive vice-president on the phone, Bill Hardenstein. He explained that they didn't have any record of a contract, or a letter of commitment, or even a file to indicate that there had been any conversation, and the sales rep was at some distant point. So I went to work on it, and before the week was over, we had the charters reinstated, and at a price that everyone could live with.''

How many people were involved?

''I've heard that about three thousand are coming by air out of California.''

One other thing, speaking of unity: word had it that Trailways and Greyhound were cooperating pretty closely here.

''Well, as you know, an awful lot of buses are coming, a lot more than Greyhound has. So, Trailways is the second largest carrier, and where they had equipment available, we gave the bookings to them.''

But there was another link, a Christian one, and it turned out that the wife of the owner of Trailways, Pat Kerrigan, was the person whom the Lord used to lead Marge Cohen into a deeper walk with Christ. What was more, her husband Jim was loaning his special executive coach, fitted out with all the luxury of a private jet, to Washington For Jesus, to bring John Gimenez and his staff up from Virginia Beach on the eve of the rally.

Hearing that, I had a funny feeling that God was going to bless both bus companies in the coming year.

10

Whited Sepulchres

Waiting out on one of the traffic islands of Los Angeles International Airport for the Rent-a-car shuttle to come along, I remembered reading that the state of California had 22 million people in it. That meant that if it were a nation separate unto itself, population-wise it would be the eighth largest nation in the world. Standing there at sundown, with all the traffic whizzing by, I felt like it *was* another country — another world, really, where women wore huge sunglasses and tight pants and stiletto heels, and men wore open shirts and gold neckchains and white patent leather footwear, and *everyone* was gorgeously tanned. Lotus Land it had been called, and considering that it was 42° when I stepped on the plane at Logan Airport, I was delighted to be standing there in a balmy 82°.

I spent the next day getting acclimatized and lining up appointments — or rather, trying to: Jack Hayford was completely tied up, and Demos Shakarian was nowhere to be found. His secretary Diane said: "Listen, if you find him before I do, would you call me and tell me where he is?"

Sunday morning, I planned to drive up to Jack Hayford's Four Square church, The Church on the Way, located on Sherman Way, in Van Nuys. I called for directions and was told that there were four services on Sunday morning. My inclination was to get up early and go to the first service, leaving the rest of the day to explore the fabled southern California beaches (when in Rome. . .), but I prayed about which one to go to, and kept getting the fourth, which did not begin until noon. It did not make much logical sense, cutting the day in half like that, but I had learned the hard way not to ignore such leadings.

Sunday turned out to be a perfect day, a carbon copy of Friday and Saturday, and the drive north on the San Diego Freeway was exhilarating. Back east, driving was largely regarded as a nuisance — something you had to do to get to work, or get the children to school, or go grocery shopping. Downtown Boston or New York or Washington were nightmares to drive in at any time of day, and to get within a dozen miles of them at rush-hour (a nebulous time period which seemed to expand to an hour and a half before and after its appointed span) was to invite disaster. Yet here, just to get out of doors and commune with nature, one did it by car. And more than a few were doing it that Sunday morning.

I got to the church on time — early enough to join the hundred and fifty or so who were waiting outside for the third service to end. I was surprised at the preponderance of young people under thirty, and it made me wonder what sort of preacher Jack Hayford was. I was about to find out; the doors opened, and we entered a sanctuary with warm brick walls and paneling, and a platform area that looked more like the living room of a home than a church sanctuary. Taking a quick look around, I estimated that the seating capacity was around 350, and every seat was filled. What was more, it looked like the ushers might be showing people to an overflow room — no wonder they were breaking ground for a new church!

Jack came out — tall, thin, angular, looking more like my idea of an early eighteenth century school master than a late twentieth century southern California pastor. He spoke a bit like a school master, too, displaying an analytical grasp of his subject and considerable erudition, though at the same time he seemed almost embarrassed of this and attempted to be "just folks," joking with the congregation, telling stories on himself, and so on. His flock didn't care; they obviously liked him just as he was, even if he did occasionally use words they didn't understand.

And when he got into what he really wanted to say that morning, I could see why. Because he, too, was one of those who was not afraid to call sin sin, and to speak to it strongly and directly. One of the things he was concerned about that morning was the whole question of divorce, and not just in general, but among Christians. It had a lot to do with what we, as the Body of Christ, had to repent for.

"It is impossible for us to live in a culture like ours without it scraping some of the sharp edges off of our discernment about values. It is amazing how much we can become used to. And all of us have suffered the pain of a sudden discovery that we're not as discerning or as sensitive in an area as we used to be. Some people call it maturity or sophistication, but what it really is, is the erosion of sensitivity."

He then applied what this process had done to our concept of marriage, saying slowly and with great emphasis: "The marriage relationship has become so damned cheap." He continued with mock facetiousness: "Well, it's nobody's fault now, nobody's responsibility. Just split and separate or separate and split." He paused. "It is a damnable trait! And that studied use of the word is to say that there is fundamentally a flow of hell that is ruining our understanding of relationships. That is not said as an indictment or judgment against anybody that has known the horrible domestic agony of a divorce. That's simply saying that we are being stampeded by horrible forces that weaken conviction and erode values. . . . There is such a cheap, rapid road to separation and divorce that is held by our society today, that it has infested the mentality of the believing Church to a phenomenal degree!''

He spoke of the antidote: letting the spirit of Christ so permeate one's home that it became the center of every relationship, husband-wife, parent-child, between relatives, between friends, everywhere. ''When sexual infidelity, adultery, comes to mean little, if anything, the Bible says that two things are happening: you're splintering your personality, and you're giving place to demonic control in a segment of your life. And I have dealt with just enough people who have eaten the sour grapes that look so sweet and found the bondage that came thereby and the pain and suffering, that I have no judgmentalism towards them. I hurt for people like that. But I am angered by the fact that the social mores of the time have so crept into the thinking of people named believers that they don't recognize that their 'house' is being dug through! You're not hearing a pastor on a tirade today. . . you're hearing a pastor, a shepherd, that's tired of seeing sheep ripped up by the wolf.''

There was more in that vein, and when he got through, everyone in that church saw with greater clarity than ever before the need to keep our discernment sharp — and the need for repentance, individually and corporately, for our part in letting things come to such a pass. Jack had confided with us that this was his favorite service, because he didn't have to be concerned throughout about finishing on time, so that the next service would not be delayed. I now understood why I was to come to this particular service, and why there were so many young people in the congregation: they *wanted* to hear it straight from the shoulder, with no punches pulled. They knew that they needed to hear about sin and repentance that way, and I suspected that for many of them, Jack was the strongest parent-figure in their lives.

After the service, I managed to see him for a moment — long enough to secure an interview on Tuesday, before I left for San Francisco. Mission accomplished — and much more than accomplished, as I thought about what he had said.

That evening, I had a chance to visit an old friend of Barbara's and mine named Carol Sobieski. Many years before, Carol had come to Hollywood to pursue a career as a script-writer. She had married a lawyer and was still happily married and had children old enough to be going off to school. She had also risen to the top of her profession, winning several awards, including an Emmy for her dramatization of Amelia Earhart. Her latest film was the Willie Nelson movie, ''Honeysuckle Rose.''

When I told her about the project which had brought me to California, she said that the producer with whom she had done a good deal of work recently had been urging her to do a major film drama on the whole evangelical scene today. Only he did not want a sympathetic treatment. ''It's been a long time since anyone has written an Elmer Gantry-type exposé,'' he had told her. ''The timing couldn't be better. I want to show where all the money goes, and just how hypocritical those people really are.''

I was not shocked by what she said; it reinforced the growing conviction I had that it was about time we Christians faced up to the fact that the world did not *want* to see us in a favorable light. The two respective systems of values had so diverged that our mere existence became an instrument of conviction in the Spirit of God — unless we could be shown to be false, and thus even less honest than non-believers who admitted to selfish or hedonistic values. If that could be done, then the threat of potential conviction would be greatly diminished, and the world would be free to pursue its chosen course without the possibility of guilt. In the old days, they stoned the prophets who would speak for the Lord; nowadays, they did it with novels and exposés and docu-dramas, which were infinitely more effective. A stoning outside the walls might be witnessed by a few thousand of that city's inhabitants. A modern multi-media assault could reach into the homes of millions.

Tuesday morning, April 15th, dawned bright and hazy, a perfect copy of Monday, the 14th, which was a perfect copy of — no wonder so many people moved to southern California! I sensed how easily I could become accustomed to such soft climes, and I could see God's wisdom in planting me where He had — on a raw, windswept corner of New England that jutted out into the North Atlantic, where the ocean temperature in mid-July was in the mid-fifties.

After a dozen phone calls the day before, I had finally tracked down Demos and set up an appointment at his house for 10:00 AM. My appointment with Jack Hayford was not until 12:15, so while it would be a tight schedule, it was feasible. In the meantime, I had an hour and a half to kill, and there was a strong temptation to roll over and catch a few more winks, or read another of the old *Time* magazines I had brought with me. Instead, I did what I knew I should do and got up and did a bunch of stretching exercises and pulled on my running gear and went outside. It was extremely muggy — though it was only 8:30 and not more than 80°, all the cars going by already had their windows up. Across from the air-port motel was a development that never got developed — paved streets criss-crossing an open field. I took an easy pace along these, and looked up to see a huge 747 settling into its final approach, wheels down, flaps fully extended — I never realized such a big plane could fly so slowly. It almost seemed suspended in time, hanging there, shimmering silver against a milky sky. I could see the passenger windows clearly and wondered if any of the businessmen, going through their attaché cases, speculating whether the rent-a-car they had reserved would be waiting for them, happened to look down and notice a lone figure running down an empty lane. Suddenly, without knowing why, I reached up and waved.

Back in the room, I showered, packed and checked out, and headed the Thrifty rent-a-car towards Downey, the suburb of Los Angeles where Demos lived. Little bits of good fortune had been dogging my heels on this trip, and one of them was the car that they had given me. I had asked for their least expensive model, which wasn't ready. The much more luxurious model I was now driving was ready, however, so they let me have the latter for the rate of the former.

The distances were a little further than the map indicated, and I arrived at the Shakarians' beautiful Spanish-style home on its small but well-groomed lawn about ten minutes late. Rose answered the door and invited me into the study, where Demos was on the phone. We had some soda together and reminisced about their son Richard's wedding a few years before which was the last time I'd seen them, and then Demos showed me into the living room, and in these formal, quietly elegant surroundings, spoke to me of things heavy on his heart. I had heard him many times before, in his role of founder and director of the Full Gospel Businessmen, but I had never been so moved by what he said.

He talked about how America had shifted away from the philosophy and intent of our founding fathers, shifting from being God-centered to being humanist. "It's very diabolical and very deceiving — in fact, from all I've learned, I would say that it would almost be anti-God, anti-Christ." What made it hard was that the humanists' intentions were *good:* they truly wanted to make a better way of life for everyone. The only thing was, they wanted to do it without God. And it couldn't be done without God. "I'm not an educated man," Demos said slowly, "but I'm a man of God, and I believe in the principles of God. I believe that God can rule an individual life, He can influence a nation. . . and He is interested in every phase of the government of our nation.''

But the humanists didn't see it that way. They felt that it was up to them to improve the quality of man's lot. ''Bootstrap religion,'' Demos called it: ''The intellectual, the man — we're lifting ourselves up. And we're putting less importance on Christ than ever before in history.''

The result was that we were in worse shape than ever before. Some months before, he and John Gimenez and a couple of others had called on a series of Senators and Congressmen, and at the end of that day, late in the evening as they had stood on a street corner near the Capitol Building, Demos had been so grieved that he wept. ''I had been to Washington many times, but never before had I had one Senator after another say: 'Will you pray for me?' They knew better than we did how serious was the underlying trouble. Looking back, I don't think they told us everything they knew — and they did know, because they would be the next to know after the President — but they didn't want to frighten us. But one Senator, Jesse Helms, did say, 'We're at the point where it's either God or the Battle of Armageddon.' ''

Demos had turned to his friends then, and said, ''America's in trouble now, and she needs us. She needs all the Christians now to rally together and pull together and move the hand of God to save America. Otherwise, she's gone. And this is what the devil wants to do: wreck this country. Because if this Christian light, which America was founded for, goes out, the whole world will plunge into darkness.'' He paused. ''From now on, I'm going to work day and night to save America.''

What were some of these problems that no humanist could correct, no matter how hard he might want to? ''The morality problem, as I see it, has gotten so big that no man can right this wrong. Only God can do it. Take divorce among Christians: it's an epidemic. What causes that? The breakdown in the morality of the nation is having an impact upon the Christian, who is getting caught up in it. It ruins the family, it ruins their lives, and yet they turn around and remarry and go on as though nothing has happened. Now, I am sure that God is a forgiving God, and I'm sure that some of those who have gotten divorced and remarried, God can forgive. But at the same time, I'm also sure that this is not pleasing to Him. . . . So maybe judgment will come at the house of God. Maybe the Christian is going to have to repent!''

He had one more comment on morality: "You know, we're crying out for leadership, 'God, raise a man to lead, raise a prophet!' But where is he going to come from, if we all have become fragmented in our Christian belief? We polarize ourselves to the point where anything goes now, God can cover up any sin, just go on. And there *is* grace, but how long will God's patience endure, even under grace?''

The subject of the letter to Mark Hatfield and others by the zealous coordinator came up, and I asked him about that. "It's not right to blame him or make him the fall guy, because he was only acting out what all of us had been talking about, back then. Maybe we wouldn't have written it the way he did, and now we have seen that God would have us steer as far away from politics as possible, but it was all of our responsibility.''

I thought of Thomas a Becket, the head of the Church of England who was murdered in Canterbury Cathedral by four of Henry II's knights, because they had overheard their king say, "Will no one rid me of this man?" In their zeal, they had taken him literally, assuming that he would be pleased at what they had done. He wasn't; in fact, he was horrified. But he took full responsibility on his own shoulders for their deed.

"I have one thing more to tell you," said Demos. "I think you ought to know my feeling about John Gimenez. God could have shown me a vision to go to Washington. He could have shown Pat Robertson, or Jim Bakker, or the Assemblies of God, or Oral Roberts, or any number of people. But God took a boy who was once in the gutter, and I've known Johnny since

1965 — that was the year we took him with us over to London, and what a story that was!''

He diverted to tell of their stay in the London Hilton. So powerful was John's ministry to addicts that they got a room and two barbers and spread a sheet on the floor, and started giving haircuts to those newly saved, cleaning them up and giving them new clothes. The hotel finally asked them to leave the premises, because more than fifty addicts had come in, and none had left. Demos took the manager upstairs and a couple of journalists to show them what was happening. They went into that room, and there were the new converts standing in line, waiting to have their hair cut, and the hair was six inches deep on the floor! Demos asked the reporters if any of those boys would let anyone touch their hair, if they weren't saved, and they agreed that they wouldn't. And with them all cleaned up and in new clothes, it was no wonder that the hotel staff hadn't recognized them when they left!

''God took this John Gimenez, who had such an impact, and had him build the Rock Church, and then had him call this rally in Washington, D.C. Isn't it beautiful that a man who had gotten so low that the doctors and psychiatrists and the police had all given up on him, saying that he would become a vegetable and die from dope, that that was the only hope he had: that he would die. And Jesus took that broken vessel and healed it, saved it, cleansed it, and today he heads up Washington For Jesus. He's the man in charge. I tell that story all over western California, because this whole thing is a miracle. And it's a story that should be told.''

I assured him that it would be.

I glanced at my watch as I drove away from Demos's — 11:35. I had forty minutes to get to the Church on the Way over roads that I hadn't traveled before. But as I drove, I found that I had, first of all, a thankful heart for the interview just completed and inner peace about the one coming up. The day was in God's hands, so I relaxed and did not push the speed limit. I was driving along the famed Hollywood Freeway, enjoying the perfect day and imagining this same stretch of #101 in the Thirties — Gary Cooper in his grey Dusenberg, Tom Mix in a Stutz, Myrna Loy in a cream-colored Packard Twelve. . . .

As I was dreaming along, I rounded a bend, and there above me was the downtown Los Angeles skyline. I shivered. The tall civic and office buildings looked uninhabited and unearthly; they had differently rectangular shapes, but they were all uniformly white in the noontime haze. And it was haze, not smog — at least, not the dingy, tobacco-stain color that I had come to associate with smog. The silvery haze made the buildings I was about to pass under appear all the more like a dream or a mirage. My flesh began to tighten on my scalp, because as I looked at the flat, black, reflectionless windows of these white buildings, they reminded me of the eyes of a corpse; in fact, I had the overall impression that I was gazing at a city of the dead. That there was no one alive in those buildings. That they were — *mausoleums* was the word that came to mind, although I had never used that word myself and had seen it only once or twice.

Abruptly, I emerged from the underpass, and it was behind me. But for an uncanny moment I felt as though I had somehow been given a glimpse of the future. White sepulchres. . . .

Once again, by the grace of God, I got to the church on time. Well, I was actually five minutes late, having gotten lost finding the office, but fortunately Jack had been detained and did not get there himself until 12:35. He was as apologetic as I was relieved, and so, to save time, we had soup and cheese and crackers in his board room.

Jack had agreed to serve on the national steering committee of Washington For Jesus at Pat Robertson's request, and it made sense since so much of the outreach of the Church on the Way was intercessory prayer. I asked him specifically about the role that an independent minister named David Schoch had played in the Four Square denomination's decision to change the date of their annual convention, since it was in direct conflict with the date of the rally.

"David called last November, and asked if he could see me, about something that God had put on his heart that he felt was very important. He came on November 20th, and I had asked Dr. Vincent Byrd and my son-in-law Scott Bower to sit in. The thing that was so beautiful about David's presentation (for our moving the dates of our convention) was his complete sense of submittedness in his presentation of an authoritative word. 'If I seem offbase,' he was saying, 'then you can completely disregard what I am saying.' It was the best form of such a presentation of an authoritative word that I've seen, the essence of a functioning prophetic ministry. The authority was there, but it was said in such gentleness and wisdom, that it was really *entreating.*" He paused, recalling it. "We were all moved, and I called John Holland, the chairman of our convention, who witnessed that it was a word from God. 'Jack,' he said, 'if you'd called any later, we would have had a financial disaster, in terms of our printing bill. But we just have time to change it.' And they did."

Did he himself have any concerns about the rally? "I am concerned that there will be some negative fallout. You can't have that many people gathering without some religious weirdos. I feel badly about that, since it only takes one kook and the camera in the right position to bring a real reproach on the whole thing. . . . I wrote to (and here he named two friends with prominent ministries in the Washington D.C. area), saying to them that I realized that Washington For Jesus could seem to be a very ominous event to people who are living in D.C. and carrying on a low-profile witness to touch especially the intelligentsia. I said that I did believe WFJ has a valid contribution to make in Christian witness, and I was close enough to the leadership so that I *knew* there was no hidden political agenda.''

I interrupted to ask him if anyone had suggested that he write such a letter, and he assured me that no, it had just come to him to do so.

''I closed by saying that, in the context of our national form of public life, I saw nothing inherent in this event which was necessarily inconsistent with Christian standards. However, this was not my characteristic style of witness, and, of course, not theirs either. The only thing was, that as a West Coast congregation, so distant from our nation's capital, I felt we could not neglect our participation in an event which was expressing the care and concern of so many in the larger Body of Christ.''

And with that, the clock struck one, as it were, and I had to leave to catch my plane to Oakland. Once more the Holy Spirit had accomplished all that was necessary, in the amount of time that was available.

Jim Coffaro was waiting, as I emerged from the exit ramp in Oakland. While we waited for my bags to appear on the carousel, he pointed over to the World Airways ticket counter. I was surprised to see a mob of people there, and looking closer, I could see the reason why: to celebrate the end of their strike (and to re-establish themselves in the thinking of transcontinental travelers), they were offering for a limited time a bonanza bargain rate to Baltimore: $69! ''And,'' Jim exclaimed, ''from Los Angeles it's only $36! I know that from our church alone a hundred people are now going who couldn't afford to go before. Do you realize that it could cost close to $300 to fly one way normally? And the Baltimore airport is actually closer to Washington than Dulles International. *And* one of the girls from our church works for World and has been able to tell us when the best time was to come out and get our tickets." He shook his head. "The whole thing is a miracle. Literally thousands of people will now be able to come from the West Coast who could not have afforded it before."

On the way to the restaurant, where I was to meet Violet Kiteley and her son David, who co-pastored a church called the Shiloh Christian Fellowship, at whose camp meeting WFJ was first introduced, Jim told me about the role he had played in getting John Gimenez and Demos together. Jim had known John since long before the latter was a preacher, and so it was to him that John turned when Pat Robertson had suggested that John also seek confirmation from Demos. Jim Coffaro was an officer in the Full Gospel Businessmen, and he knew that Demos was in Brussels, but was returning to Washington, so he flew to Virginia Beach, and he and John flew up to D.C. together. On their way to Demos's hotel, Jim had said, "Wouldn't it be beautiful if, as we walked into the hotel, the first person we'd see would be Demos?"

"Brother, if that happens," John replied, "it would be a sign from God."

It did happen, and that was the night that Demos made his commitment.

When we got to the restaurant, I was introduced not only to the Kiteleys, but to a young red-headed New Zealander named Rob Gwynne, whom God had brought half-way around the world, apparently to help with the West Coast public relations effort on behalf of WFJ. They had had some remarkable successes — interviews on radio and television all over California, mostly on secular stations, as it turned out, because so many of the Christian stations were reluctant, because of

denominational hassles.   The fact that Rob was a New
Zealander, and was given a gift of holy boldness, seemed to
open doors that might not have opened otherwise.

Rob gave an example which had happened recently.
"There was this cable station down in San José, and Jim and I
were scheduled on it.   Actually, it turned out that they were
over-scheduled, and then the host who was supposed to be
doing the interviewing was sick.   When the station called me,
they said that they might be able to straighten out the over-
scheduling, but they had no host.   'Well,' I said, 'what do you
have to do to be a host?'   They explained, and I thought, well,
the Lord is bigger than anyone else out there, so I said,
'What's to stop me from doing that?'   Nothing, they said, and
so I called Jim and told him that I would be interviewing him
about Washington For Jesus."   He laughed.   "They had a
hundred thousand subscribers on that cable, and we had our
own half-hour TV show.   When they replayed it on the air that
evening, we got four calls about going to WFJ, and the whole
thing cost us nothing."

Rob added, thoughtfully, "But you know, it's sad:
whenever I'm on one of those live, call-in shows, the question
I'm most often asked is: 'How come I haven't heard about this
before?' "

I asked Violet and David then about the night that this had
all come into being, and they shared in filling me in.   It all
began at a camp meeting of their church in July of '78.   They
had a good turn-out, around a thousand people, and John was
the guest speaker.   He told them that he had had a burden for
some time, one that he hadn't even shared with his own church
yet.   And he prefaced it by telling them about a Christian who
was recently traveling on a train, when, in the seat ahead of
him, two men got on board, already intoxicated and drinking
from a bottle they carried with them.   The drunker they got,
the louder they got, and the filthier became their stories and
their language.

The Christian began to pray: Lord, close their foul mouths!

Stop that flow of garbage! But nothing happened. If anything, the drunks seemed to carry on with more gusto than ever. Finally, the Christian could stand it no longer. How come, he said to God, angrily though inwardly, I'm praying, and you're permitting that demonstration for Satan to continue? And when he had finally calmed down enough to hear God, what he heard was: *why don't you have a demonstration of your own?*

He thought about that a moment, and almost rejected it, because he had an abhorrence of drawing attention to himself. But then he stood up and started to sing, "Glory, Glory, Hallelujah!" in a good, loud voice. The two men in front of him looked up at him in astonishment. "What are you, drunk or something?" they asked him. But he ignored them and just kept singing, and drowned them out, and pretty soon other people in the train car started joining in. "Mine eyes have seen the glory of the coming of the Lord!"

That was when John put the challenge to them: "Why don't *we* have a demonstration for God? Why don't *we* let the whole world know that the Church of Jesus Christ is still alive and cares?"

A thousand voices responded with cries of approval, and that night a vision was born.

It was to go through some rapid evolution out there; it started out to be a festival, with a choir of ten thousand, and an orchestra of five hundred. From the speakers' platform, David Kitely nominated John Gimenez as chairman of the festival, the others on the platform seconded it, and the congregation signified their approval by shouting "Aye!" and cheering. Initially, it was going to be in California, but it was Violet Kitely who felt very strongly that it was supposed to be in Washington, D.C. After all, John had been preaching on David, and hadn't David aimed for Goliath's forehead? So the venue was shifted to Washington, and national confirmation was sought, and the rest was history.

As we drove to their church, I asked the Kiteleys if they had encountered any major areas of resistance, and I was surprised at the answer: "The biggest resistance we've gotten from large churches everywhere is, 'We have an Israel tour planned for this year.' So we've been trying to tell people that this year our own Jerusalem needs us. It's ironic, but if Washington For Jesus had been in Jerusalem, instead of D.C., I think we might triple the turnout, from California anyway."

But fortunately, a lot of Christians *were* making Washington their Jerusalem this year, and I met one outside of their church, a good-looking black lad named Don Lewis, who was their youth director. He told me about Youth With A Mission's West Coast project, for which they had been training young people for several months, and with which he had been assisting. "They are going to be sending out buses of young people at various times, prior to the rally. They're going to drive across the country, stopping in towns and cities along the way, and infiltrating them with the Gospel of Jesus Christ. They'll stay a day, maybe two, then get back on the bus and move on towards Washington."

I was excited by the idea; it reminded me of how the great kings of medieval England used to raise armies to defend their coasts against invaders from France. Only now they were going to raise an army of Christians!

11

In the Phone Booth

"In a few minutes, we'll be landing at Washington's National Airport. We want to take this opportunity to thank you for flying Piedmont. . . ." As the stewardess's well-modulated voice continued, I checked my watch: four-thirty on the afternoon of the 17th. Which afternoon was the 17th? I had forgotten what day of the week it was, and to my surprise, it took time for me to work out that it was Thursday. Up to that moment, I had been mildly contemptuous of people who bought watches that gave the day as well as the date. Who on earth couldn't remember what day of the week it was? Me.

The plane landed smoothly and began to taxi up to the gate, and I was almost sorry the flight was over. I had occasionally heard heavy-traveling evangelists speak almost wistfully of that two- or three-hour respite aloft — a flight was an oasis in the sky, with no one to talk to and nothing to do but catch up on correspondence or sleep. One man I knew wrote most of his books five miles up in the air. But if I had ever been envious of the life of a traveling evangelist, I wasn't any longer. I'd had enough of a taste of it to realize that instead of broadening one's horizons, it progressively narrowed them, until one's days became an endless series of airports, church suppers, meetings, motel rooms, hurried breakfasts, loading baggage into the trunks of waiting vehicles . . . and coming home with a suitcase full of dirty laundry, to face a desk full of mail and bills. And magazines — the pile of news magazines on the night table had grown so large that I must be about three months behind. Well, maybe I would take them with me on the next flight . . . .

In the meantime, I would try to make up for all the lost time at home, by doing as many "family" things as possible in the few days at home — a bike ride with Barbara and our daughter Blair, who was thirteen and growing like a weed, a picnic, dog obedience school, going out to get fresh doughnuts for breakfast, a walk on the sand flats of Cape Cod Bay. . . . This last trip home, I was greeted by Blair with exciting news: our community's band would be marching with the Massachusetts contingent in the WFJ parade! Blue-and-white uniforms were being given a last-minute going over, people were memorizing Sousa, and there was even drill practice on a softball field, so that the band would execute a smart "column left." The route would begin on Madison Drive on the Mall, turn left on 7th Street, left again down Constitution Avenue, left on 14th Street, and a final left onto the Mall and the dispersal point . . . .

"Please remain seated with your seatbelt fastened until the plane has come to a complete stop. . . ." Other men in the cabin were ignoring the stewardess, and I was tempted to do likewise, but what was the hurry? I'd only have to wait at the baggage carousel. I was staying with some friends in Alexandria, who were expecting me for supper, after I'd rented a car, and they were familiar with airport delays, so there was no great urgency. So I sat in my seat, and with a feeling of satisfaction polished off another old *Time* magazine.

That night I learned to my chagrin that, as far as local Washingtonians were concerned, the rally was still one of the best-kept secrets in the capital. Virtually nothing had appeared in the *Post* or the *Star* in more than two weeks. The next morning, the couple I was staying with left early for work, and since I had an hour before it was nine and I could start calling, I drove down to the Potomac, to run a few miles on the bike path. It was cool, for a change (the temperature had dipped down into the 60's), and the remains of a ground fog hung over the Mt. Vernon parkway. I parked at the upper end of the path and started down at a comfortable pace, glad to see that the sun was already burning off the fog. It shafted down through the overhanging branches, as if through the highest windows of some vast cathedral, and I noticed how quiet everything was. Then I heard the sound of a cardinal singing, and though I looked all around, I couldn't see him. I did see a squirrel up ahead on the path, however, as he scampered around the bend and up a convenient tree, to observe my passage from the safety of an upper limb.

All at once, I caught sight of the river, flat calm and burnished silver under a low-lying sun, and then I was on the flat and running over a boarded trestle, looking out over a river so wide I could barely make out the opposite bank in the morning haze. A couple more miles brought me out into a beautiful green park, and now I could see the Washington skyline shimmering in the distance, like Dorothy's first glimpse of the Emerald City. Grinning, I circled the park, then headed back up the path to the car. It was uphill now and more work, but I felt so peaceful inside I scarcely noticed. There was the squirrel again, and this time he chattered at me for disturbing his foraging.

After showering and dressing and having some orange juice and cereal, I sat down by the phone on the table in the living room and stared at it — for half an hour. I was here to interview Senators and Congressmen regarding their response to Washington For Jesus; to do that I had to call their offices and make appointments. Yet here I was, paralyzed with faintheartedness. I regarded the phone as if it were a black, coiled serpent, ready to strike at my hand, if I dared reach for it. And all the while, I rationalized furiously: well, no office got fully functional much before 9:15 — 9:20 — and then the first thing a Senator did was go over the day with his appointments secretary, which would take another fifteen minutes or so — 9:45. . . Finally, I screwed up all my courage and made my first call. The young lady who answered couldn't have been more gracious: she was afraid that the Senator's appointments secretary was at that moment in his office; could I leave a number, and she would get back to me?

Instantly, I realized several things: I shouldn't be conducting my business out of my friends' home, although they had encouraged me to do so; I didn't have a secretary to receive incoming calls, while I was making outgoing ones; and if the Senator's secretary already had a number of calls to return, there was no telling when she would get to mine. There was only one thing to do: go into Washington, and call from there. "Um, no, I, uh, am going to be moving around today and won't be at this number; it would be easier for me to call back. When would be a good time?"

"Well, the Senator is going to be on the floor this morning; why don't you try right after lunch?"

And so I got in my car and headed for Washington. On an impulse, I drove to the Mall, to see if they had started work on the speakers' platform, and incredibly I was able to find a free parking space on Jefferson Drive, near the Smithsonian. It was an absolutely gorgeous day on the Mall, and as I strolled over towards where some workmen were putting up chain-link fencing for the enclosure, I heard the tinny wheeze of a carousel, playing "The Farmer in the Dell". . . .

There was a phone booth on the main floor of the Cannon Building, one of the three Congressional office buildings adjacent to the Capitol, and it was unoccupied. Armed with a fistful of change, I sat down in it, stacked the coins on the little shelf, balanced my briefcase on my lap, and cradled the phone to my shoulder to make the first call — as I'd seen countless salesmen do. (Considering what they charged for local calls in hotel rooms these days, Ma Bell's four-foot-square, eight-foot-tall offices were the only place to do business, for anyone not on an expansive expense account.) I made the first call, and another, and another, and gradually the piece of paper I was writing on filled with notes: "Appointments secretary named Elaine — still out to lunch — press secretary is Brad — he, too, out to lunch — call back 2:45 — called, Senator on the floor for a roll call, then tied up — possibly Monday morning — call Monday at 9:00. . . ."

Finally, after an hour and a half, the phone booth got so cramped and hot that I had to take a break. I swept what was left of the change off of the shelf and into my pocket, and got up to stretch. Strolling up to the Capitol, once again I was struck by the evanescent beauty of Washington. Carefully land-scaped flower beds were blooming in bursts of color, and the Japanese cherry trees were covered with their magenta blossoms. Even though it was nearly four, the temperature was still up in the high 70's, and there were flocks of tourists on the Capitol steps, some having their pictures taken, others just sitting and resting. Up the drive came four Marines, running in bright red shorts and cut-off sweat shirts, while a whole Cub Scout pack in their blue uniforms was being herded in the opposite direction. And above it all flew the Stars and Stripes, so bright that it looked like it was ready for a Technicolor movie. Just at the corner of the Capitol, I caught a glimpse of the Washington Monument in the distance, silhouetted in the late afternoon sun, which would soon be setting behind it. I couldn't get over how peaceful it looked, like a visual bene-diction over the city — in spite of the low level excitement that seemed, at times, to emanate from the very pavement of Washington.

Inside the Capitol Building, there were tourists everywhere, buying postcards, taking pictures, asking questions, admiring the sculpture and architecture, and hoping to catch a glimpse of a face they recognized. There was still time to make a few more calls before everyone closed up shop and went home for the weekend. I asked a young guide where I might find a phone, and he directed me to the basement, specifically to the docking area of the shortest underground railroad in existence, that gave the senators a chance to make it from their offices to the floor of the Senate for a crucial vote. (Apparently Congressmen were considered younger and/or more fit, or possibly just less important; anyway, they got to hoof it.) At the end of the platform were two phone booths: one was a regular pay phone, and the other was labeled "In House Calls," and had no slot to insert coins. Curious, I inquired of the train dispatcher and learned that the latter enabled one to call any Senate or Congressional number — free.

I thanked him and was glad that I had worn my dark suit and resembled one of those aides who were always striding purposefully, wherever they happened to be going. I strode purposefully over to the In House booth and tried a call. Eureka! After a few more calls, however, it became obvious that the dynamo of democracy was winding down for the weekend, and so I called it a day. I had yet to confirm a single appointment, but I was getting closer. I had also learned the secret of successful lobbying: don't push.

There were times when, as I was shunted off to a press secretary or an aide, frustration would well up inside me, and I would want to say: "Listen: a week from now there'll be a million people on your front lawn, and they'll be there because they are mightily worried about the state America is in. And a big bunch of them are coming from your boss's state, and each one's a voter, and there are probably a hundred more just like him back home that didn't come but feel the same way! Now, are you going to let me —"

But that wasn't the way, and I knew it. Even if I did get

through, God couldn't possibly bless it. So, instead I would pray for the Lord to open the door, if He wanted it opened, and would say that I would be glad to talk to anyone, but obviously for quoting in a book, no one but the Senator would do. And it paid off. Monday morning, back at the In-House phone, bright and early, I noticed a change. After the third or fourth call to the right aide or secretary, by the grace of God maintaining patience and good cheer, I discovered we were beginning to develop a relationship. I could appreciate the immense pressures that they were operating under, and they in turn, began to feel sorry for me, eventually making exceptions that they might not ordinarily make. I began to get appointments. (Later, I discovered that I had done phenomenally well, considering that I had no letters of introduction, no lead time, and no one going to bat for me — except the Lord, who of course was all anyone needed.)

My first interview was Tuesday afternoon, with House Majority leader Jim Wright of Texas. I was surprised at the spaciousness of his office, and how tastefully it had been decorated — emerald green carpeting, gleaming old wooden desk and tables, tall windows flanked by cream-colored draperies. . . . it bespoke dignity and graciousness, as it had for more than a century. Congressman Wright seemed a down-home type, to use an advertising phrase which I detested because it fit so well. He motioned me to a wing chair and sat down in its twin, alongside an antique drum table. As I fumbled with my tape recorder, he waited patiently, and with a sickening lurch in my stomach, I realized that I really hadn't prepared any questions. "Uh, well, sir, I don't know how many people are coming next Tuesday, but what do you think about all that?" Oh brother, if that wasn't the dumbest opening to an interview —

But he didn't seem to notice at all. He knew what I wanted, even if I didn't. "I think it is appropriate that we come together as Americans and express our gratitude in humility, lest we become too proud, lest we arrogate to ourselves the assumption that we're wealthy and enjoy these blessings due to our own innate goodness. . . . A Scripture that has meaning for our time is in the eighth chapter of Deuteronomy: 'When thou hast eaten and art full, take care that thou shalt bless the Lord thy God for this good land that He has given thee, for it shall be that if you do at all forget, and follow after other gods and bow down before them and worship them, I testify against you this day that you shall surely perish.' " He paused and looked at me. "I hope that may never be the epitaph of our civilization."

How did he feel about some of the problems that were besetting the country just now? "Maybe those problems have been set upon us as a means of testing our mettle, of refining the gold that is in us. Of reminding us of our deep and profound reliance on Almighty God. . . . A nation is free, if its people are worthy of freedom. God deals with us in the realm of the unenforceables, and that's the difference between a free people and a slave people. He doesn't put us in jail, you know; He doesn't tax us. What we do, must be done in a voluntary way. . . ."

And then he said an extraordinary thing, which reminded me of what Demos had said. "Let me ask you, as one public official, that you pray for us. That our judgments be wise. We are frail, fallible, mortal human creatures. We do not possess wisdom of Olympian prophets, nor the sanctity of saints, and we, in the words of the old spiritual, stand in the need of prayer. My plea to you would be: that your people pray that God's wisdom may permeate the institutions of Government, that God's purposes may work through the duly elected representatives of the people, of both parties and persuasions. That you try to cultivate a totally non-partisan outlook and attitude. That you uphold everyone and condemn none. If that's done, its effect has to be good. It can't be bad. And perhaps, in that mysterious way which defies our human understanding, it will work its way through to even some of us who are not aware that we're being prayed for.''

I thanked Congressman Wright, and as I left, I had the curious feeling that God had blessed him with that office, and that he knew it.

I took the elevator downstairs to the subway platform — not to use the phone this time, but to ride over to the Russell Building. It was a short ride — all of about four minutes, which was a good thing, since I was due in the office of Senator Bill Armstrong of Colorado in fifteen. Shown a seat by his receptionist, I glanced at the door of his inner office, and saw a Washington For Jesus poster. I discerned that this was going to be a positive interview.

Bill Armstrong was a tall, well-built, disarming fellow in shirtsleeves, with black metal-rimmed glasses. He had a way about him of making you feel relaxed and not self-conscious in his presence, and we got right to it. How did the Senator feel about the possibility of a million people showing up next week to pray for the nation and its leadership? ''Well, I'll be pleased if a million show up, and I'll be pleased if a hundred thousand show up. In fact, I hope that the possibility of a million coming hasn't been overplayed, so that if there's only a hundred thousand, that will seem like a small number. After all, a hundred thousand is a lot for a football game, let alone a prayer meeting. And I think from the Lord's perspective — and I don't mean to be presumptuous about this — if a hundred thousand come, as Bill Bright might say, 'in the spirit of Jehosaphat,' that will fulfill His requirement. What matters is the condition of their hearts, not how many there are. When the Lord was on the verge of destroying Sodom, which, I think, is a fair comparison to the United States, He did not say that He would save Sodom in the event that a certain number of people turned out for a rally, or that they elected a majority of believers to the Sodom City Council. What He said was, if there were fifty righteous men, He would save the city, or forty or thirty or ten, and so on.'' He paused and thought a moment. "I think that the test of America's future will not be found so much in numbers of believers, but in the quality of their belief and the faith to which they've yielded to these purposes.''

How did he feel about America today? The Senator pointed out that, since coming to Washington, he had also come to Christ, and was thus considerably more optimistic about America than he had been. He summed up his feelings with a rather graphic picture: "I can't remember which historical character said it about which other historical character, but it applies to America today: it's like a mackerel in the moonlight; it both shines and stinks.''

He gave an example of what he meant, describing the view from his hotel window, the evening before he was to attend a prayer breakfast in Las Vegas. Seeing my raised eyebrows, he added, "Well, the Lord did command us to preach the good news to all nations, and He didn't specifically exclude Las Vegas. There was a broadcasters' convention out there, and in real life I'm a broadcaster, so that was my connection with it . . . . Anyway, as I stood at the window about six floors up, looking out over that tremendous expanse of neon light, it was beautiful at sunset . . . a testimony at once to the creativity and at the same time the depravity of human beings. That's a long answer to your question, but that's how I think of America today.''

On Friday morning, as I transferred my base of operations into Washington itself, I turned the car radio on and first learned of the aborted rescue attempt of the Iranian hostages. There was an unusual number of black limousines pulling up in front of the Capitol, and slipping into the now-familiar phone booth, I made a few more calls and discovered that the entire Hill's weekend plans seemed to have been affected by the morning's news. Then, at eleven, I presented myself at the office of Orrin Hatch of Utah.

Well-groomed and reserved, the Senator noted that, in the wake of the rescue attempt, the rally couldn't be coming at a better time. "We're in grave difficulties right now. Our families are being attacked by various forces in our society. Our individual children are being beset on all sides by humanism and other programs that are literally designed not to increase their belief in God, or their belief in spiritual matters. We have all kinds of legislation coming through Congress that is detrimental to the family, and to the country as a whole. . . . Still, I'm an optimist, though. . . I think we have much going for us, but we're going to have to change the Congress to pre-serve our land."

What did he mean by "change the Congress"?

"Well, we have a lot of people who believe in the enhance-ment of the federal government, versus the enhancement of the private sector. And I believe we have a majority here who believe that the federal government is the answer to all of our problems, when in fact, a great number of us believe that the federal government has been the principal *cause* of many of our problems. . . over-regulating, over-legislating, and interfering in so many formerly private-sector matters. Right now, we are considering legislation that would allow the federal government to step between a husband and a wife, between parents and their children, and would promote all kinds of debilitating societal responses."

What role did he feel an awakened church could play?

"America will always be free, as long as America is good, and the way to have America good is to have that which has always made America good, remain strengthened: the fervent belief and faith of the American people in their respective reli-gious approaches. I'm talking about our Judeo-Christian ethic, which has dominated America all of our lives."

Did he see that influence ebbing now?

"No, I think our people are just as strong as ever, but for

some unknown reason, the majority of our people have become lethargic and not participated in the democratic process. . . . We have allowed the loud-mouths and the detractors of our society to have too unchallenged a say. And we have failed to stand up in one of those areas where we really need to stand up, but I see that changing.''

I thanked the Senator, and left his office, hoping that he was right. I hurried to my car, to listen to Defense Secretary Brown's press conference on the rescue attempt, and then got a bite to eat. Suddenly realizing how tired I was, I noted again how many people were sitting on the grass in front of or alongside the august granite edifices, making picnics of their brown-bag lunches, or simply dozing. It was another sparkling, unusually warm day. . . . Finding an unclaimed bit of shade under an old oak next to the Library of Congress, I shed my suitcoat, and using my briefcase as a pillow, stretched out for a catnap. Half an hour later, remarkably refreshed, I went back to the phone booth, where I spent the remainder of the afternoon.

That night, John and Dean arrived, and we spent most of the evening bringing each other up to date. Outside, the weather had begun to deteriorate. A low pressure front had been forecast, and with it the likelihood of several days of bad — more typically April — weather. We stayed up too late talking, as usual, and as usual after a late night, I woke up considerably earlier than I had intended. *Go back to sleep* was a command that I never seemed to be able to get through to my engine room, so after a few minutes, I slipped out of bed and donned my running gear and went outside. Mercifully, the all-night downpour had temporarily slackened to a heavy mist, and I headed for the Mall, about a mile and a half away.

As I approached it, I could see clutches of rain-soaked, miserable-looking ''No-nukes'' headed in the same direction. They looked as if they had been up most, if not all of the night, and I wondered if any of them secretly wished that they were home in bed. Judging from their number, the Task Force's projection of a tenth of the figure that their promoters were projecting was going to prove generous. I passed some, and they seemed friendly enough, but when I approached the corner of 14th Street and Constitution Avenue, I came upon a bunch of eight or so that were dressed alike, in army blankets with white sheets over them, as a priest would wear a surplice. They were barefoot, and under their scraggly hair their eyes burned with a gleam that I had not seen since the bad-acid days of the late-Sixties. As I passed by, one of them called out to me: "You can't get to heaven by jogging, brother!"

I tried to think of a quick comeback before I got out of range, but typically couldn't, and spent the next couple of miles mulling over and discarding possible retorts. And then, as the mist became a little more solid, I thought of the perfect riposte: "If you know so much about heaven, how come God is raining all over your parade?" But abruptly, imagination became imminent reality, as I rounded the next corner, and there they were again. Should I — no, conscience clamped my mouth shut. I passed by in silence, and unnoticed, as they were heckling some other "straight" who was walking his dog. It occurred to me later that, although everyone was praying and believing for good weather Tuesday, what if God rained on our parade too?

By the time I got back, John and Dean were up, and after breakfast we made our way down to the Mall. The WFJ command vehicles were in place — one for transportation logistics, and one for communications. There were four incoming phone lines in the latter, and every one of them was in use, as John and I entered. In the front of the vehicles, Janet Keim was going over the list of who was to receive staff passes, and in the back, at the end of a long table, Jerry Kantowski sat, flanked by assistants. Jerry was very calm, very unflapped. From the sound of the phone conversations going on around him, everything was about to collapse, yet the more the pressure built, the calmer he seemed to get. It looked like once again, God had the right man in the right place at the right time.

"Jer," Cush said to him, holding his hand over the receiver, "the stuff has arrived, but without a forklift, we're dead. The guy over at Thompson's can get us one, but he wants cash."

"Most of them do," Jerry replied, and I remembered him telling me that the people who service rallies had often been stiffed, when it came time to settle up. "We don't have that much on hand, and since it's Saturday, we're not likely to get it, until Sister Betty gets up here from the church."

I looked in my wallet, saw that I had three twenties, and offered it to him, if that would help. And John standing behind me, had another forty. He nodded thanks and told Cush to tell him to bring the forklift over. "But Jerry, we don't have anyone here who can drive it."

"Never mind, get it."

When it quieted down a bit, I switched on my recorder and asked Jerry if he would describe this morning's crisis.

"I'd like to direct that question to Sam Tolbert," Jerry deadpanned, nodding to the black man in the orange sweat-shirt sitting next to him.

"Sam Tolbert is this morning's crisis?" I asked with mock incredulity.

"I think Carol can handle this one better than I can," Sam said thoughtfully, looking across the table at Carol Owen.

"No," said Carol, "Jerry's really the one to tell it," and all eyes turned to the man at the end of the table.

"Okay, you really want to know?"

I nodded. "Well, we're trying to get some workers down here to finish putting up the choir seats on the speakers' platform, and to get the port-a-johns in place, wherever they are. And we have just heard that the flagpoles for the platform are on their way — or rather, were on their way: the truck they're on has just blown out its muffler in Philadelphia.

Meanwhile, there are three tractor-trailers here right now, only we can't unload them, because we don't have a forklift — which is where you came in." He grinned. "As you can see, we are still totally dependent on God for miracles."

"It does tend to keep one needy," I agreed.

Just then, Carol, on the phone, broke in. "It's Sister Betty, out at the airport. Bart was supposed to be meeting her."

"Is this *Saturday?*" Bart Pierce exclaimed, his eyes widening. "Oh, no! Tell her I'm really sorry, but she's going to have to get a cab."

I glanced at Jerry who was observing everything with such detachment that it might as well have been on his TV set. I shook my head. "You know," I said to no one in particular, "if it gets any more intense around here, Jerry's going to fall asleep."

During the next lull, Carol told me about an 87-year-old lady from Indiana, who had decided that she was going to attend Washington For Jesus, even though she had only enough money for a one-way ticket to Virginia Beach, where she checked into the Y. The Rock Church folks absorbed her into their group, housed her in a Christian home, and put her to work with the others on the final preparations. She was as happy as can be, and really being a help.

The next lull provided me with an opportunity to talk to Sam Tolbert, the man responsible for putting the TV coverage together. "My involvement with this came as a complete surprise. When they wanted to do a network-type TV coverage of the whole affair, Pat said, 'Okay, I'm with you, but I want you to take my engineer with you.' And then he told me, 'Sam, get with them and make it happen.' When they got done with all their meetings, and all their plans, some of them wanted as many as thirty-eight cameras to cover the entire parade route and the whole works. And I said, 'Fine. It'll cost you a million dollars.' And everybody said, 'What? A million dollars! We don't have that kind of money; this isn't NBC.' Well, after a lot of months and a lot of meetings, we've been able to bring the total shoot down to $150,000, which is a miracle in itself. We'll have a camera up in the Monument, a camera on the Capitol steps, one up on 7th Street, and five in the general area of the speakers' platform.''

He went on to explain how everyone was pitching in: Jerry Rose, of independent Channel 38, had been a great unifying force; Trinity was donating the satellite time for the entire twelve hours; both PTL and CBN would have cameras and crews there; a church in Dallas donated a mobile editing suite — the list went on and on. And the beauty of it was that for this one day, the only call letters that would be seen on a camera or other equipment would be: *WFJ.*

''We're trying to unite a group of Christian organizations to do a TV operation here, and as of right now, we still haven't seen half their equipment. There is always the possibility that some will not be able to supply what they have promised, and there are a lot of contingencies which still have to be taken into consideration. . . but nonetheless we're looking at a miracle taking place. Because at this point, with no money in the house and this much done, we are sitting in the middle of a miracle!''

Sam seemed to have the same kind of grace under heavy pressure that Jerry had. ''That's what you have to have. If you get all rattled and upset and all, you won't be able to do God's work. And not only will you not be able to do His work, you won't be able to do man's work, either.''

As the tempo again picked up, I slipped next door to the transportation headquarters to see how Francis Owen was doing, and found another example of cool-headedness under fire. Buses were now frantically calling in for travel and parking instructions, long after it was too late to mail them a registration packet. What was going to happen, when they showed up here unregistered?

''They can pay the $6 parking fee and $7 for shuttle bus service on the spot, and if they say that they've already sent it in, we'll just trust them as Christians and go ahead and register them.''

He looked at a piece of paper on his clipboard. ''Here's something that'll interest you: some guy just pulled in from California. He said that all the way across the country, he was passed by vans and caravans of cars, all with WFJ bumperstickers on them, and all waving to him.''

Just then, there was a knock at the vehicle's door, and Carol opened it. A long-haired boy in scruffy jeans and an old T-shirt looked up at her and asked, ''Are you here with the people who are coming for the Jesus rally?'' His face was red, and it looked like there were tears in his eyes.

Carol went out to talk to him, and came back a few moments later. ''He had come with the No-nukes,'' she explained, ''and he said that it suddenly dawned on him that they didn't have the answer to anything. It turned out he was terrified of annihilation, and somehow he knew we did have the answer.'' She laughed. ''He kept saying, 'Are you sure you're not going anywhere?' He said he was going just for a moment, to get his sleeping bag and his guitar off their truck, and he wanted to make sure that we'd be here when he came back.''

It was the first defection of what we hoped would become a tide.

12

The Eye of the Hurricane

Sunday morning, D-Day minus two, was a rainy, grey, clammy repeat of Saturday morning. At the command center on the Mall, with less than forty-eight hours to go, the pressure had escalated till Jerry looked like he might doze off at any moment. I wondered how I would function in his shoes, and decided that it was a good thing I wasn't in them; I would undoubtedly be tempted to take action myself, and would wind up leaving the command center in order to do my own trouble-shooting. Which would have been precisely the wrong thing to do.

A wise general, in command of a military operation, had one predominant responsibility: to be available to make the decisions that only he could make. That meant he could not be out in the action, leading his men, no matter how much he might want to be. Nor was this the time for any drastic revision of strategy; the time for changing the plan of attack had passed weeks before. Once the operation had been launched, it took on a life and momentum all its own. And yet, if the planning had been thorough enough, all would be well.

Someone had once likened the planning of an operation like Washington For Jesus to riding an elephant: you started off, and the elephant began to walk at a leisurely pace. He was easily guided then; a prod behind the ears with the driver's stick was enough to turn him whichever way you wanted him to go. But gradually he gained momentum, and it became increasingly difficult to administer course corrections, until finally he was lumbering along at full gallop, crashing through the jungle at breakneck speed. There was no guiding him then; all the driver could do was grab the elephant's ears and hang on for dear life!

Washington For Jesus had reached the galloping stage. And yet, for all that, there was still an uncanny peace about the command vehicle. One sensed that it was very much under God's grace and protection, as well as being mightily girded in prayers from all over the country. It was a little like being in the eye of a hurricane.

"You'll be interested to hear what happened to our defector," Jerry said, hanging up the phone. "We found him some young Christians to stay with, and last night some Youth With A Mission kids led him to the Lord! Today he's sticking to them like glue, I hear. Doesn't want to take any chances on losing what he's found."

At that moment, two other people in the vehicle began speculating on how many people actually would show up, the day after tomorrow. As that happened to be everybody's favorite vain speculation, we all joined in. "It seems like every time we uncover a rock," Jerry chuckled, "we find another five hundred unregistered buses." He noted that the prevailing estimate around the command vehicles was about half a million.

"Well, I don't want to be a skeptic," I said, noting the skeptical tone in my voice, "but I had a dream Thursday night, in which I asked that question, and the figure that came to me in the dream was 350,000."

Jerry chuckled. "You're not old enough yet to be dreaming dreams; you're still supposed to be seeing visions." He looked out the window. "But for what it's worth, I had the number 385,000 come to me two weeks ago."

Dean and I went to see how Ronn Kerr and his wife Jo were coming in the two prefabricated press buildings, which were each about the size of a house trailer. "Not too badly, all things considered," said Ronn, in answer to our query. "The electric typewriters haven't shown up yet, so Jo is having to make out the first press credentials in longhand, but otherwise things are looking pretty good."

How was the coverage shaping up? A week ago, he had been extremely enthusiastic, despite the lack of lead time. Late April had looked to be pretty quiet, news-wise, and so the media were beginning to take a real interest in the rally. The "Today" show had gone so far as to schedule a three-day in-depth series on it. But now, with the fast-breaking developments in the abortive rescue story, all network camera crews which had been assigned to cover the rally had been withdrawn and held in reserve, for any last-minute angles that might emerge. "All non-essential news coverage has been can-celled," Ronn concluded with a sigh, "and it looks like the rally is non-essential news. Conceivably, we could be back on their shoot schedule by Tuesday, if this Iran thing quiets down, but I'm not holding out much hope."

Before we knew it, it was noon and time to meet with our photography team. Finding a quiet corner in the old Smithson-ian building directly behind the speakers' platform, we gath-ered round and laid out our strategy. Dean and John and I would be carrying hand-held recorders, to capture as much color and spontaneous interviews as we could. I would concen-trate on the speakers' area, while the other two worked the crowds. Dan Ford, John Sorensen, Luke Norman and Ev Sahrbeck would be our photographers, assisted by Paul Moore. I would be taking pictures as well — I felt we would need at least a thousand good shots to choose from.

At 1:30, I bid our team adieu and headed for the airport, where M.R. Welch's plane would soon be dropping Anne

Gimenez. I was going to hop a ride with them back to Virginia Beach, to be at the Rock Church that evening, when several planeloads of rally-goers from Puerto Rico and Hawaii arrived. John Gimenez had anticipated that the service would be exceptional, and an ideal kick-off for the rally, and he had suggested that I fly down, and then fly back up to D.C. with him, after the service.

The night before, however, Dean had asked me if I really felt that I was supposed to go to Virginia Beach, especially in light of the fact that the rest of our team would be assembled for the first time. Shouldn't we all stick together on the eve of the 28th, especially since we were responsible for bringing the team there? But I was insistent; I was expected, and I wanted to go.

The sun broke briefly through the heavy overcast, just before I left for the airport, and I took that as a sign of God's blessing. I ignored the fact that by the time I had reached the airport, it had clouded over again. M.R. and Red Carter, another seasoned pilot, arrived on schedule, but before we took off, M.R. advised me: "You should know that there's some weather building up south of us."

"Bad enough to cause delays?"

"Not yet, but it could."

"What do you think?"

M.R. looked over at Red, who shrugged. "There's just no telling. We're going to go, and if it works out, fine; we'll have Brother John back up here before midnight. If not. . . ."

I made my decision. "Let's go." As soon as the plane was gassed up, we took off. No sooner had we left the ground than we began experiencing turbulence. The weather radar showed unusually dense storms on either side of us; in fact, we seemed to be flying down a narrow corridor of comparatively moderate weather. There had even been tornado warnings to the west of us, though M.R. and Red both felt that the corridor would hold up until we got to Norfolk.

It didn't. Norfolk closed down within thirty minutes after

we took off, so we diverted over to Richmond, to sit and await developments. It was a strange afternoon. The sky directly above us was clear blue and sunny, with fluffy white clouds scudding across it, although periodically there would be the oddest sunlit rain showers. It was hot and muggy and very calm. To the east, across the vast open field in which the airport was situated, dark cumulo-nimbus clouds towered thirty thousand feet in the air, as breathtaking as any picture I'd ever seen. The sky to the west was even more ominous — solid black thunderheads, moving towards us. "Weirdest weather I've seen in all my years of flying," Red commented. "There's just no accounting for it."

We obviously weren't going anywhere very soon, so I took a walk, to figure out what to do next. There was no telling when the small plane might be able to get to Norfolk, let alone get back out again, or if Washington would be operational when it did. They had just told me that John Gimenez would ride up in the special executive coach that Jim Kerrigan, the owner of Trailways, had loaned Washington For Jesus. There was one hitch: the bus wasn't leaving until 4:00 in the morning, and so would not get in until at least 8:00, and I had two appointments on the Hill tomorrow morning, which I couldn't take a chance on missing. In the meantime, the weather around Washington was deteriorating, and there was a growing possibility that it would close down behind us.

What now, Lord? But as I walked along, there was no answer, not even a nudge, and I began to sense that God was not very pleased with me. I figured that I had better find out where I had gotten out of His will, or I would never hear anything. I didn't have too far to look. My place, right then, was to be with the team that we had assembled to cover the rally, and not just for fellowship but to forge a real bond, as all of us would soon be taxed to the limit. God had tried to warn me, first through Dean's check, and then through the weather, but I had turned a deaf ear. Nor had I prayed about going; I had wanted to go, and thus had automatically assumed that it *must* be God's will — a rather arrogant assumption, in retrospect, and an indication that my head had expanded a size or two.

I set about to see if there were any flights left back to Washington. There was one, a rag-tag commuter airline, leaving in just barely enough time to get on board. Saying goodbye to M.R. and Red, I ran for it and got the last seat. The plane was an old, boxy, high-wing, twin-engined affair, the sort that the British had put in service in the early fifties, for super-cheap Cross-Channel flights. Half-way to Washington, we began to encounter the worst turbulence that I had ever experienced, in a large plane or small. We were being slammed around on all three axes — roll, pitch and yaw — and outside in the roiling black clouds, frequent jagged shafts of lightning illuminated first one side of the plane and then the other. People began to be sick, and I began to be scared.

In all my life, including a couple of thousand hours of Arctic flying as a radar officer in the Naval Air Force, I had never been afraid in an airplane. Anxious, yes, on occasion when we would lose an engine, and I could remember one instance out of Iceland, that we had lost two and were in danger of losing the third, when I was more than anxious. But even then, I was not scared — not like I was now. I could feel cold sweat rolling down my sides, as I sat gripping my armrests and staring rigidly straight ahead. Under my breath, I rebuked Satan, the author of fear, but for the first time in my ten years with the Lord, I had no confidence in my authority as a blood-bought child of the Lamb. And I knew what the matter was: I was afraid of dying out of God's will. In any other similar situation, like being trapped in an elevator last fall for an hour, I would be aware of His grace and would experience His peace, even in the face of possible death. If God chose to call me home then, well, so be it; it was His decision, and He was in charge.

But there was something different about this time. Though I prayed and pleaded and repented, I could not regain that sense of closeness to Him. I was out of His will to have flown; I might have gotten even further out of His will by impulsively grabbing this last flight back. I could have rented a car for less than the ticket cost, and the trip on the ground would have taken only an hour and a half longer. . . .

A terrific thunderclap shook the plane, while at the same time lightning lit up both sides of the cabin at once, which meant that it was directly above us. Was it my imagination, or were the cabin lights starting to dim? I looked at my watch: fifteen minutes to go — if we made it. I felt my own stomach beginning to rise up, but mainly I felt the icy grip of fear on my heart. There was nothing to do but sweat it out.

Looking around the cabin, I could see that the other passengers were of the same mind. No one was speaking; they were all staring straight ahead, eyes unblinking, like a cargo of zombies, faces white, neck muscles rigid, lips pale and compressed. Undoubtedly we had passed the Point of No Return; all we could do now was barrel on through and hope that the old crate held together. Another burst of lightning showed the wing on my side actually flapping. I wondered what more than twenty-five years of metal fatigue had done to the bolts that held it to the fuselage. And then we began to go down.

But we were descending, not diving, and we broke through the clouds at about five hundred feet and banked to line up on the final approach. There was still rain, and still a gusting cross-wind, but it began to look like we were going to make it. The plane flared out, the wheels chirped twice as we bounced and re-established the surly bonds of earth, and in a few more moments, we had arrived at the gate. I had been on airplanes where, after a difficult landing, the passengers applauded the pilot and flight crew. There was no applause this afternoon; ashen faces were still stretched taut, as we disembarked.

My friends were surprised at my early return. "Did you see the rainbow and the fantastic sunset?" they exclaimed, when we finally got reunited. No, I hadn't seen it. Nor did I tell them what I had seen — about my being out of God's will, and the harrowing flight home.

Monday morning, the 28th, I awoke once again to the sound of pelting rain. That made three mornings in a row. But even had it been clear, I had no intention of going out running; I was still tired, and we faced the prospect of two long, gruelling days, with about three hours' sleep in between, if we were lucky. There was no point in expending unnecessary energy.

I had to face the fact that I was down, mentally and spiritually, and I had a pretty good idea why, and what to do about it. My opportunity came at breakfast, and I told Dean and John of my willfulness the day before. "Well," Dean said, shaking his head, "you should know yourself well enough by now, to know that you've *got* to pray about a thing like that, especially if someone else questions whether you're supposed to do it. Your problem is, you don't like hearing it from anyone else."

I nodded. "I'm going to start listening a lot more carefully," I agreed. "I'm sorry that I haven't been."

Dean clapped me on the shoulder. "Forget it," he said gruffly, "we've got work to do."

John was typically well organized that morning: "Dan is going with me, when our Arizona delegation calls on Congressman Rhodes, to take photographs. Dean will meet you at Senator Jepsen's office at 11:15, where you have your last appointment. You will go directly to National Airport, where you will be picking up Pat and Shirley Boone, whose plane gets in at 12:29. Dean will drop David off at Constitution Hall, and take the Boones on up to their hotel, where he will wait and then take Pat to his rehearsal and then to the White House at 5:00 for Rosalyn Carter's presentation on behalf of Cambodian

Relief, and then out to RFK stadium. Meanwhile, Dan and I will join David at the women's meeting at 1:30, or thereabouts.''

After breakfast, feeling considerably brighter, even if the day wasn't, I grabbed a cab to the Cannon Building, where I had an appointment with Congressman Larry MacDonald of Georgia. A big man with a big smile, I liked him right away. Did he think the rally was going to accomplish anything?

"I think it will be certainly helpful, but I hope that Christians will take it far beyond that. I hope this will be the very beginning, not the termination of what will be viewed as a national project. Because Christians who are not knowledge-able are very gullible and easily seduced by secular humanists, and that is true of many, if not most, of their ministers.''

How would he describe the spiritual state of America right now?

"Grave.''

Then how did he feel about our future?

"Well, if you go by the past, never in history has a nation gone to the directions or to the level that we have and survived. When you go as far as we have down the road towards destruc-tion and degeneration, there's no parallel in history where a nation's come back. Now, having said that, I don't believe that that means you cannot come back. I think it *can* be done, and I think it is our opportunity and obligation to try to do it.''

What would it take?

"It's going to take the development of an informed elector-ate. It's going to take an energizing, for lack of a better term, of God's people who have been apathetic, who have been ignorant, and in some cases frustrated, but in virtually all cases lacking in knowledge. . . . The fifth chapter of Isaiah, thirteenth verse, says: 'My people are being led up into captiv-ity because they lack knowledge.' Most ministers, most funda-mentalist, Bible-believing Christians are not knowledgeable. They do not understand the Biblical basis of our morality, upon which our laws are based. Many of them are led to believe that they have no obligation to be concerned with the affairs of contemporary times. They have not read the admonitions of the New and Old Testaments on this point. Many of them feel that they don't even need to worry about getting registered to vote; many of them are just sitting around, waiting to be raptured. They'd better wake up, because they are going to be held accountable. . . .''

I commented that many Christians seemed to feel that as long as they were in right relationship with God, there was no need to dirty their hands in politics.

"But they're *not* in right relationship with God! God very clearly gives us a command to bear witness to uphold His laws, and when we allow the legal basis of our society to be eroded from a Biblical basis into humanism, into atheism, as the basis of our laws, we are *not* fulfilling that witness, and we are not fulfilling our charge. It makes no difference how sanctimonious we would like to appear! A lot of people say that you can't legislate morality. It's the height of stupidity to say that, because all law is *morality enacted.* The only question, therefore, is: what is the basis of morality? Is it going to be a Biblical basis? Or is it going to be a humanistic basis, towards which we are actively drifting?''

No one had summed it up as dramatically, but there it was. I thanked Congressman MacDonald, and headed for the underground passageway and subway over to the Dirksen Building, for my last interview, with Senator Roger Jepsen of Iowa. I must have looked like I knew where I was going, because a lost tourist plaintively asked directions. I stopped, pointed the way to her, and continued striding purposefully to the subway.

When I got to the office, Dean was just arriving, with a tall, lean gentleman in a three-piece suit, whom he introduced to me as Don Townley, of Dallas. It turned out that Don was the security agent assigned to Pat Boone, and he would be going with us to the airport. We admired the pictures on the wall, many of the Senator with his fellow colleagues, including one of him and several of his colleagues in sweatsuits and running shoes. Just then, the receptionist showed me in. The Senator waved me to a chair opposite a desk piled with work, and I asked him how he felt about what was going to take place tomorrow.

"I think it's very fitting and proper in these times of trial and tribulation that we have now, that, as the nation's capital, we again seek the guidance and the blessing of God Almighty, and reaffirm our dependence upon Divine Providence, confessing our individual and corporate sins, and coming to Him in prayer and worship. We can set an example, not only for our nation, but for the world."

How did he feel about America's spiritual and moral condition right now?

"I think there's a rebirth of a spiritual awareness in this country. You can almost feel it daily, that a spiritual re-awakening is taking place. . . . I, of course, have personally experienced in the past several years this rebirth of an awareness of Jesus Christ — what it means in our individual daily lives to give one's life to Christ, and to purposely and practically live that, every day. People of all walks of life are coming to the Lord these days on an accelerated basis, so I'm encouraged by what's happening."

We talked some more, and I thanked him for his time. Going with the others to the car, I shared with them what he had said. If he was encouraged by how many people were coming to the Lord now, I was encouraged that we had some Senators and Congressmen who were willing to testify that He was indeed Lord of their lives.

Dean picked his way through the noon-hour traffic, and at that point it looked like we might get entangled, but we slipped free, found just the right parking place in short-term parking, and were at the arrival gate fifteen minutes ahead of the Boones' arrival. Passing the time, I said to Dean, "You know, Barbara gives me a hard time about not keeping my work area neat. She ought to see the offices of some of the men I've interviewed — papers and files and books and clippings stacked everywhere!''

Dean chuckled. "How else are their constituents going to know how hard they're working?''

Don Townley did not join in. Although he was courteous and polite, it was obvious that he already considered himself on duty, even though his charge had not yet arrived. His appearance was relaxed enough to the casual observer, but his eyes were wandering everywhere, checking out all the people coming and going, the people like us who were waiting, even the airline personnel — no one escaped his idle scrutiny. What was more, he stayed on duty all that day and the next — a credit to Executive Security Consultants of Johnson City, Tennessee. And so, Dean and I read the paper, while Don read the crowd, until they announced the arrival of Eastern Flight #133.

We put our papers down and watched the exit through which Pat and Shirley would emerge — and watched and watched. More and more people came out, until finally there was just a trickle, but no well-tanned movie star and his striking blond wife. Well, maybe they were staying on board until the other passengers had cleared the area, to minimize the commotion that always eddied around celebrities in public places. But when the last straggler exited and still no Boones, I began to get a little anxious. Finally, I hurried down the ramp and on to the plane. There was no one waiting in the first-class section, or anywhere else. "Were Pat and Shirley Boone on this plane?'' I asked one of the stewardesses.

"Sho' nuff,'' she said in a honeyed southern drawl. "He sat right heah. But Miz Boone wasn't with him; he was alone, and he was the first one off.''

I dashed back up the ramp. "We've missed him!'' I called out to Don and Dean. "He's traveling alone!'' Instantly Don went to call his superiors, while Dean went to the Eastern counter to have Pat paged. I stood still and prayed like mad. Washington For Jesus had planned to send a limousine for the Boones, but I had volunteered Dean's Cadillac instead, as I figured it might be the only chance to get an interview with him. And now I had blown it, but good! Calming down, I got a nudge to check the baggage claim area. And there, standing all alone with four bags and a wardrobe trunk was Pat, smiling, patient, and not the least bit concerned that apparently no one had come to meet him.

I introduced myself, apologized for being late, then hurried off to find Don and Dean, which I was able to do before they completed their own missions. In a few minutes, we were all aboard and headed for Washington, while I had my tape recorder unlimbered. Did Pat think the rally was timely?

"It's long overdue! I wish to goodness it was an annual event, and maybe it will be, after this. I guess the largest single bloc of votes in the country, outside of male/female distinctions, are Christians. And yet, we're not exerting nearly enough influence on every level of government. . . . This is a Judeo-Christian society, founded on the Ten Commandments and the Sermon on the Mount. Our Constitution, all of our leaders — they never foresaw that we could become so concerned about separation of church and state that we would totally divorce Christian considerations and Christian influence from our government processes."

How did America feel about itself?

He thought a moment before answering. "I think we've become a hypochondriac, troubled, ailing and deeply worried society. We're fearful, and the only force greater than fear is faith. And faith can only come from a person's sense of relationship with God, who's in control." He paused. "I think it's time for this sick society to call in the Great Physician, which is what this is all about, and simply say: we *do* need divine help. We *do*, as a people, recognize that we don't have the answers to our serious ailments, and therefore we'd better all truly try to become again one nation under God.''

We were pulling up in front of Constitution Hall, where I would be getting out. But before I did, there was one more question: what sort of reaction did he anticipate nationally to tomorrow's rally?

''It will cause shock waves. . . . Already we see lots of people who consider themselves pragmatists or just 'balanced citizens,' fearful of the influence of dedicated Christians in government, or in our national policies. They really wish that we would just keep on doing what we've traditionally done, at least in the last couple of generations, which is just go to church and stay quiet. And allow a sort of amoral establishment to continue to dictate our policies, and to gradually take away the constitutional rights to worship and assembly and to vocal influence — a very real influence in government that Christians and Jews in this country are supposed to have and are guaranteed.''

With that, I got out and waved goodbye, as they hurried up 18th Street. Turning to the white stone building beside me, I went around to the basement entrance we had been shown the previous month, and checked in with the security guard. Upstairs, the auditorium was already filling, though the meeting would not begin for another hour. Anne Gimenez, with Vonette Bright's help, had assembled an impressive roster of speakers. Bobbie James, wife of Alabama's Governor Fob James, would say the opening prayer and would be followed by Vonette, Shirley Boone (who had arrived on an earlier plane), Dale Evans Rogers, and Ann Kiemel. Then Sarah Jordan Powell would sing, and would be followed by Senator Jepsen's wife Dee, Anne Gimenez, Senator Strom Thurmond's wife Nancy, Congressman Frank Horton's wife Marjorie, and Pat Robertson's wife, Dede. The final, keynote address would be delivered by Iverna Tompkins, WFJ's national women's coordinator.

The speakers gathered in a small meeting room for prayer,

while in the auditorium a sense of expectancy was building. By two o'clock I could not see any vacant seats, though there was still half an hour to go. Just then, John French and Dan Ford arrived, and I learned that the Arizona prayer presentations to Senator DeConcini and Congressman Rhodes had gone extremely well. According to John, both men seemed touched that so many people were actually going to be praying for them every day they were in office, and they were glad to have the delegation pray with them there in their offices.

Promptly at 2:30, the speakers took their seats on stage, and Bobbie James came to the lectern to pray. At this point, I had to make a decision regarding the book. Though I was going to record every speech, there was no way I could possibly include transcripts of them in the book. Nor could I comment on each one of the dozen speeches that afternoon, the two dozen that evening, the entertainers and speakers at RFK stadium that night, and the more than five dozen slated for the Mall tomorrow. I decided I would comment only on those things which struck me as truly unusual.

For instance, about a third of the way into the afternoon program, Ann Gimenez, who was emceeing, was handed a message: apparently there were some five hundred women outside who were unable to get seats, and had no loudspeaker system through which to follow what was going on inside. Ann was an old hand at packing churches: she'd had to do it often enough at home. Informing the audience of the predicament, she invited them to participate in the solution. "I want to see hands of anyone who has a vacant seat beside them. I can see some down front here on the left," she added, pointing to the area that had been reserved for the press, "and maybe some of you younger ladies wouldn't mind sitting on the steps in the aisles, so that we can get everyone in who wants to come in."

Somehow, it was done. And crossing the stage to take a vacant seat now, came a woman with almost regal bearing, dressed in a blue suit with a white scarf. This was Dee Jepsen, who opened her remarks by saying, "It's good to be here; I was one of the five hundred!" Something else she said stuck with me: soon after she met the Lord, she prayed much as all new Christians do, "Lord, I'll do anything in this world that You want. I'll go to Africa." In the stillness of her heart, the Lord spoke to her of her then-unsaved husband: *This man is your Africa.*

It was also a surprise to learn that Dale Evans Rogers was a grandmother sixteen times, and a great-grandmother four times. And that Ann Kiemel, who had started running only eight months before, had already run in three marathons, the most recent being Boston. She shared a little about that, and how she had to pray through every yard of the last four miles. I had new admiration for the courage that was there, behind the sweetness. And Iverna Tompkins struck a resonant note, when she said that while Shirley Boone had spoken of wives as the heart of the family, she also saw them as the backbone, for it was the wife who held the whole family together.

But if I had to pick one anecdote that made the deepest impression, it was a story Nancy Thurmond told about a note that a teenage boy, Johnny, left for his mother, after doing his weekly chores.

> Dear Mom,
>   For picking up my room every day and picking up my clothes: 25¢.
>   For cutting the grass and raking the leaves: 50¢.
>   For running all your errands, Mother: 25¢.
>   For doing all my homework and not getting into any trouble at school: 75¢.
>   You can leave the money in my room.

Nancy then recited the note that that godly mother left for Johnny:

Dear Son,

For bringing you into the world: no charge.

For washing tons of diapers, and every pair of pants, every shirt, and every pair of socks you ever wore: no charge.

For sitting up nights when you were sick, adding wrinkles and gray hairs every time you cut yourself or broke your arm: no charge.

For giving you, son, the best years of my life: no charge.

P.S. I love you.

13

A Lion in Winter

I glanced at my watch as I left Constitution Hall — 4:40. I had twenty minutes to get over to the Press Club for the dinner for the principals. That was just enough time to walk it, which was a good thing since there were no cabs in sight and rush hour was well under way. The weather was cold and damp and gloomy, and while it wasn't raining just then, it felt like it would be starting again at any moment. Certainly the heavy overcast confirmed the forecast of still more rain, with no end in sight.

Walking up 17th Street, I was suddenly stopped in my tracks by the sound of multiple wailing sirens behind me. Turning, I saw in the distance, crossing the ellipse, six motorcycle policemen leading a fast-moving convoy of Secret Service vehicles, in the middle of which was a black limousine, with more motorcycle policemen bringing up the rear. In a moment they were out of sight, their sirens more a memory than an echo.

Astonished, I turned to the man next to me: "What was *that?*"

"President," he said disinterestedly. "He must be coming back from Houston."

I recalled reading in the paper that morning that the President had gone there to visit some of the burned survivors of the rescue attempt, but I was surprised at the attention his entourage drew to itself. When I thought about it, though, it made sense. There were two ways that the Secret Service could get him from Point A to Point B: high profile or low. Low profile would mean camouflaging his presence, possibly even to the extreme of disguising him and his car, and having only one or two men to guard him. High profile meant that instead of moving him incognito, they made no attempt to hide him — plenty of protection along a varied route at a high rate of speed. The sound of all those sirens and those lights flashing and the fast pace had the cumulative effect of momentarily paralyzing those nearby — and in that moment, they were gone.

I arrived at the Press Club just as Ted and Louise Pantaleo did, and as we rode up in the elevator I asked Ted how it had gone with the delegations. "People reported back to me today that as they met the Senators and Congressmen, again and again they were asked: 'What do you really want?' 'Why are you here?' And the delegations kept answering, 'All we want to do is pray with you, and show you the love of Jesus,' and they said that they'd never been exposed to that kind of thing. But every one of them prayed with their Senators and Congressmen."

We were given directions to the room where the dinner was being given, and as we walked down the hall I passed by a door that was propped part-way open with a standing cigarette urn. From behind the door I heard someone say, "Jacks or better to open."

People were just beginning to arrive for the dinner, and I was glad to see that the headquarters staff was there, as well as more nationally-known preachers and their wives than had probably ever been assembled in one place before. I had a chance to talk to Jerry Kantowski, whom I hadn't seen since Sunday morning. That was only a day and a half, but it seemed like at least a week. Jerry said that Sunday afternoon on the Mall the wind and rain built up to about 60 miles per hour, almost a tornado, and had torn down all the bunting and decorations. The rain was coming down in sheets, and the workers whom they had contracted to put everything up were extremely unhappy about it. But the Christians were out there with their hands up in the air in the middle of the storm, praising God the whole time. And when the rain stopped, the sun broke through and gave the most gorgeous double rainbow that Jerry had ever seen, right over the Mall and over the White House.

People at the dinner filled the tables to overflowing, and it was a case of family-hold-back, because more people had come than they had dinners for. I didn't completely hold back, because we would be fasting the next day, and the buffet salad looked awfully good. David DuPlessis was there, and it was good to see him again. He seemed older and smaller than I remembered him, but the twinkle was still there — God's leprechaun was still a long ways from retirement.

The spirit of the dinner was, in a sense, like a gathering of spiritual forces on the eve of a major battle. Aside from a run-down of transportation arrangements and the distribution of security passes, there would be only two speakers at the dinner: the two program co-chairmen. Pat spoke first, and now, addressing this smaller group of leaders, nearly all of whom were friends of his, he spoke more candidly than I had ever heard him. "You know, as we begin to think about what is going to be done tomorrow, it is my firm conviction that unless we see God Almighty move in a dramatic sovereign way, we are lost as a nation. . . . Consider for a moment what we are up against: Do you know that three of the top ten industries in the USA are controlled by organized crime? Gambling, pornography and narcotics — we have made them three of the top ten industries in terms of the dollars spent . . . and we, as Americans, have permitted it to happen. They have enormous money to corrupt whomever they feel like in government, to spend millions of dollars of black market money and undercover money, siphoned off in businesses.''

And then he turned to another index of America's desperate moral plight: "How many of you saw that program that CBS did on Gay Power, Saturday night? I don't know if any of you did see it, but it was one of the most sickening things that I have ever seen in my life on television. It showed how the gays in San Francisco humbled Mayor Diane Feinstein, forced her to retract a statement she had made concerning the gay lifestyle being at variance with the established norms of our society — she had to apologize for that.'' He went on to describe some of the other things she had to do, which were broadcast on television into millions of American homes over a national network. "I couldn't believe it! If God doesn't judge San Francisco and any place else that permits that, God is going to have to rebuild Sodom and Gomorrah, apologize personally to them, and then set them up with impunity for the rest of their lives. You can't believe this goes on in our country, but it does.''

What could we do? "We're looking up to one Source — we're looking up to God Almighty. And we're saying: God, we believe You. And that this land was framed by men and women who loved You, and we are their legitimate heirs, and we are going to call our nation back to the dream of the Founding Fathers.'' He looked around the room. "You and I have been chosen by God for such times as this. And brethren, it's a noble cause, and we'll look back in history and say, 'This is the day when we met in the nation's capital to intercede for the nation.' All I can say is, God bless every one of you who is participating tomorrow. But please be in an attitude of prayer, an attitude of solemnity; it's going to be a holy congregation, and we need to pray for one another.''

Pat was followed by Bill Bright. "I've come, as I trust all of you have come, with a deep sense of anticipation, for I truly believe that tomorrow could be the most important day in the history of our nation since its founding. Never in the history of this country has there been a gathering such as we're anticipating tomorrow. In fact, as far as I know, there's never been a gathering ever, where so many people of such diverse theological views have come together in the spirit of love and unity to say, 'O God, help us.' "

And then he had a word of wisdom concerning the need to keep the focus on God, and not on issues per se. "I was asked yesterday in a television interview: 'Are you here to talk about lobbying against homosexualism or abortion?' And I said, 'Look: the real issue is to clear up the spiritual bloodstream of America. These are only boils on the body politic.' If we eliminate homosexuality and abortion and all the rest, we still wouldn't solve the problem. We're here to confess and repent, to turn to God. He's the only one who can help us. And as we speak, each one of us must be sensitive to the fact that not everyone holds to our particular theology. But we all love Jesus Christ."

With that, he suggested that those at each table join hands in prayer. "Holy Father, in the name of Your risen Son, we've come together to worship and adore You and confess our sins and the sins of the nation. We've come to call upon You for a great outpouring of Your Holy Spirit upon us, that we may experience true revival and turn from our wicked ways. Thank You, that when we deal with the basic issues, the boils will be healed, and we'll see a new birth of a nation, born by Your Spirit. We ask this now, for Your great glory and honor and worship and praise, in the holy name of the Lord Jesus."

We raised our heads, and Bill added, "One final word before other announcements are made: I was privileged to visit the women's meeting this afternoon. . . . When I went into the meeting, they had begun to pray and sing praises to God, and there was an incredible spirit there — I began to weep." He paused. "And I'm a Presbyterian!" Everyone laughed.

And then he did something no one was expecting: he asked

Jesse Winley to say a word. "I'm not going to preach now," said the grizzled black warrior, "I'll do that later. This is warfare," he said in a low voice, "and tomorrow, if the enemy tries anything, like throw an egg, throw a tomato — throw a bomb — remember: we're going as lambs in the midst of wolves. The devil would love to get us to panic and run and scream. If anything should happen, let us stand. This is God's way. If we die, let us die on the Mall. When we get beyond the fear of death, Christians, we will be dangerous!"

That was certainly a sobering word, I thought to myself, as I left to go back to Constitution Hall. It had never occurred to me that anything like that might happen — and yet, of course, it could. Satan would be furious about the prospect of what would be taking place on the Mall tomorrow. Still, I had the feeling that Bishop Winley had spoken prophetically — not for tomorrow, perhaps, but for a time in the future, a time when Christians had better be prepared to look death in the face, unafraid.

It was raining outside again and I gladly accepted John and Caroline Gilman's offer of a ride. We were a good half-hour early, but already the hall was packed. Walking around the lobby, I was dismayed to see some young women passing out literature that was promoting someone's Christian-political ministry, and another man was passing out his own Christian material. Washington For Jesus had given assurances that *no* individual ministries would be promoted, and that there would be no politicizing of the rally. Yet here were these people taking advantage of the situation, with their own egos thrusting themselves into prominence. It was a shame. When they were asked to desist, the young women did so and apologized, but not the man. He was incensed and started spewing his venom over anyone who would listen to him. Fortunately, very few people paid any attention to him, and I was reminded of what Jack Hayford had said, that in a gathering of this size, there were bound to be a few religious weirdos on the fringe.

Inside the hall, however, it was like old home week! In the space of a dozen minutes, I saw at least a dozen pastors whom I hadn't seen in months or years. But, as usual, the time mattered not at all when Christian friends were reunited. And all over the hall, similar re-unitings were taking place; I never saw so many people hugging one another in one place in my life!

Dan Ford and John French had seats in the front row, and had saved me one, so I got my equipment in order — fresh batteries and tape cassette in the recorder, a new roll of fast film in the camera. Since there was no question of using a flash, I would have to bump it to double its normal speed. That done, I got caught up on how it had gone with them during the day. With enthusiasm, they described their visit to the office of the House Minority Leader, Congressman John Rhodes of Arizona. John had led the Arizona delegation. "We began by explaining why we were there, that we were not there for any negative purpose, or to promote anything, but rather just to stand with him and the other leadership of the country, believing that God was the one who could heal our country through them, and to unite ourselves in Christ for that purpose." John paused. "He appeared to be quite moved by that; in fact, he said a couple of times, 'This is an extremely humbling thing for me.'"

Dan added, "When John had prayed, and David Everett, the spiritual coordinator for Arizona, had prayed, then Congressman Rhodes prayed. He thanked the Lord for bringing all the people there, and acknowledged that God was the only answer, and the only source of the wisdom that he so badly needed." Dan's own eyes filled as he recalled the moment. "I was really impressed with his humility as a person, and his concern for the country; it was every bit as deep as ours, and he did know that God was the only answer."

John chuckled and told a story on himself. "We were going to give him a plaque, with II Chronicles 7:14 inscribed on it, but the girl who was supposed to bring the plaque to his office got tied up in traffic. Fifteen minutes into our meeting with him, she had still not arrived, and I was more worried about that plaque than about what was going on. Finally, I realized that the Lord had to be in charge of it, and not me. I was finally able to turn it over to Him, and a minute later, in came the girl with the plaque."

John Gimenez and Pat Robertson were scheduled to be the masters of ceremony this evening, and right at 7:30 John got up and introduced the welcoming speaker, a black bishop well known in the metropolitan Washington area, Smallwood Williams. "I'm thankful for the fellowship of this hour and of this occasion," he said, and I gathered that he'd experienced a few embraces himself. "As a representative of Washington, D.C., for more than half a century, I have witnessed many visitations and councils of nations and demonstrations and marches on Washington. But this Washington For Jesus rally is something else! This is history!" And for the first time that evening, there was thunderous applause. "This is a date with destiny. This is another promise. This is a different revelation. This is not a political, philosophical, economical, social meeting. This is a *prophetic* meeting!" There were cheers now, and I thought, well, they've pushed off the toboggan and we're underway!

Bishop Williams was the first to quote II Chronicles 7:14, but he was hardly the last; at least half a dozen of the speakers who followed him repeated it. And the cross-section of those speakers was a reflection of the uniting work of the Holy Spirit that was already underway. Among them were Father Michael Scanlon, president of the University of Steubenville and one of the leaders of the Catholic Charismatic Renewal; James Kennedy, pastor of probably the largest and certainly the fastest-growing Presbyterian church in the country; Bishop J.O. Patterson, spiritual leader of more than three million American blacks; and co-keynoter James Robison, whose powerful depiction of what was happening to the American family accurately expressed what all of us felt in our hearts, and whose dynamic delivery brought the entire assembly to its feet. In a quieter vein, we were equally moved by the simple but profound prayer of Ben Haden. My respect for this soft-spoken, unassuming Presbyterian pastor was to grow substantially during the next twenty-four hours.

Pat was supposed to be sharing the master of ceremonies responsibility this evening, but each time John Gimenez urged him to take over, he would smile and shake his head and insist that John keep on. I doubted if many people noticed that, but it was indicative of the utter lack of ego and jealousy that I had witnessed among the leadership of Washington For Jesus.

On balance, it was a tremendous occasion with a wealth of excellent speakers, but there was no question that the shining star of the evening was Jesse Winley. It was his finest hour, and it may have been the most telling preaching he had ever done, for it was he who set the tone for the evening, and perhaps for the Mall tomorrow. (It was with shock and grief that we were to learn, just a few weeks later, of his going to be with the Lord. All who were there that night would never forget it.)

"I just want to let you know," he said in slow, measured tones, "in case some of you are shaking — that God isn't in any trouble!" There was laughter, then roars of approval, and up on the stage, the two men who were enjoying him the most were Pat Robertson and Bill Bright.

"God has no problems — He only has *solutions*. He's God Almighty! He's President for life! *You didn't vote Him in — and you can't vote Him out!*" Thunderous cheers stopped him, and the men on the stage stood up, applauding, as did the entire auditorium. "He's not just king — He's King of kings!"

More cheers drowned him out.

He went on a bit on that and then said, "As Christians, we have to be de-programmed — out of our ideologies, our dead theologies — and re-programmed into God's concepts. It's not what *my* denomination says, or *my* organization says, or *my* bishop says, it's what 'Thus saith the Lord!' " and he thumped his Bible, to more cheers.

"You know, as soldiers of God, here we are in the midst of battle, and look how the devil has deceived the Church! In the midst of battle, we are out there arguing about the validity of the Word. Listen here: when you are out on the battlefield, facing the enemy eyeball to eyeball, *that's not the time to worry about what caliber your bullet is!*" Gales of laughter greeted the funniest line of the day, and then we were on our feet again, cheering.

There was more, and then he said: "Thus saith the Lord: I will pour out my Spirit on all flesh. Hear that? The great I AM is saying: I *will*. And He's going to pour it out on *all* flesh — the flesh of the murderer, the flesh of the homosexual, the flesh of the lesbian, the flesh of the crooked politician, the flesh of the up and out and the down and out. It's going to be poured out on Red China, it's going to be poured out on Russia, it's going to be poured out on Africa. And God said, it is going to be an outpouring of *conviction!* From that point on, they become responsible as to whether or not they receive the Gospel, but they're going to know that Jesus is the Christ!" More cheers, wave upon wave of them.

There was more, and we wished he could have gone on all night. But then he said, "I'm finished." And as he started to leave the podium, he turned back and said: "Here, Church, take the limit off the atonement. God spoke to me these words: there should be no sin on earth that the Church can't handle. Because Jesus has already borne it in His body on the tree. Sin past, sin present, sin future has been atoned for. Let's go on as believers and bring back our glorious Saviour to this earth. *Let us be one!* That's not going to be in spiritual heaven; it's going to be on earth! I was talking to a physicist. He said these words: The thing that causes the explosion of the atom is not when it's split; *it's when the atoms come together!* We have begun as of today an explosion in America, and when all Christians get together, we're going to blow America apart!''

He did turn away then, and the sound of applause and cheering was deafening. Bill Bright just took both of his hands, speechless. John Gimenez came over and gave him a big hug. And then the bishop did an extraordinary thing. In the middle of this stupendous ovation, he went over to his chair, dropped to his knees, and bowed his head in his hands on the seat of the chair. There were tears in our eyes, and we could have gone on applauding all night.

At length John stepped to the podium, and as the audience quieted, a woman up on the balcony began to speak forth in tongues. John held up his hand to still her and gently but firmly said, "No, sister, that is not the Holy Spirit. That's not what the Lord is doing at this time." The program continued and the moment was soon forgotten. But I was glad that it had happened, for it showed the evangelicals that the charismatics meant to honor their commitment.

All too soon it was over, but John Gimenez was much too wound up to think of sleeping, and so I caught a ride with him out to RFK stadium to see what had been happening there. It was very cold and misting, as we drove along, and judging from the size of the puddles there had been a torrential downpour while our meeting was going on. I shuddered to think of RFK, whose seats were for the most part unprotected.

I asked John what impressed him most about the meeting. "I feel there was a real spirit of unity there, and *a desiring for unity.* The price has been paid by a lot of people for this occasion, and now there's no turning back. You've got some prominent evangelical leaders who have gotten out of the boat, so to speak, and gotten on the waters, and of course, you've got some of your charismatic and Pentecostal leaders who've said, we're ready. They're throwing in the chips, and we're ready to go all the way. . . .''

When we got to RFK, I ran into Dean Smith and John Sorensen almost right away. Apparently it had rained so hard out there that everyone who was present felt like they had been through a baptism together. In fact, Larry Tomczak had even called it that, as the rain had drummed down on the umbrella that someone had held for him, while he shared his enthusiasm for what God was going to do tomorrow, and was already doing in their midst.

As usual, Dean had noted the little details that brought the scene to life for me, as he talked. ''It was already misting heavily when I got here and people were getting wet, but they were mostly young people, and they didn't seem to mind. Even when the mist turned to out and out rain, I saw only two raincoats in the whole place, and one of them was mine. People were inventive, though; I saw a lot of them wearing plastic garbage bags with holes torn in the top, or rather bottom, depending on how you looked at them. And people with baseball caps would have water dripping off the ends of them. Over the stage, there were great sheets of plastic to protect the pianos and sound equipment, but it wasn't too successful. The pianist in a group called the Lamb no sooner touched the keys than they all collapsed — so he quit. But by and large there's been a very good spirit here; everyone's bearing up remarkably well.''

How many people were there? ''Well, a little after 9:00 the scoreboard said, JESUS - 30,157, DEVIL - 0, which sounded like a pretty good score.''

John Sorensen added, ''When they started shouting Jesus is Lord, over and over, it got so loud the whole place seemed to shake. The only other comment I would make is that there seemed to be some confusion among some of the young people as to why they had come: some said it was for a celebration,

others thought it was to pray for the nation, and still others said
it was to repent for our sins. I heard a few arguing about this,
but mostly people were just enjoying the evening, in spite of the
rain.''

And then he remembered something that had happened to
him that afternoon. "You might be interested in this: I met
some people in the Hawaii contingent, and they told me how a
woman in their party had been promised a plane ticket, but it
hadn't worked out and she was really sad. The travel agent
said,'Come on over anyway, and we'll see what we can do; we
might even take up a collection for you.' Well, she went, and
United Airlines has this Tic Tac Toe game that the passengers
play: if you get three in a row, you get a free round-trip ticket
anywhere. This woman was the only person to win the game
on the Honolulu to San Francisco flight. But that wasn't all:
she was also the only person to win on the San Francisco to
Chicago flight, and on the Chicago to Norfolk flight!''

"Come on, John, that's a little — "

"No, it's true! It was told to me by Roy Sasaki, a United
Methodist minister from Kahuku." He checked his notes.
"Others in the group were Reverend William Ah You, state
coordinator for Hawaii, Reverend Woodrow Yasuhara of the
First Assembly of God church, and Tuigamala Eddie Laulu,
Pastor of the Central Samoan Assembly of God church.''

"Okay, okay, I believe it. It's — "

"They sang 'Aloha' on the Capitol steps, but with Christian
words, an original composition by Brother Blair from the
Assembly of God church in Maui.''

Laughing, I went out to the stage, where the carbon arc
lamps were still shining down, illuminating the raindrops as
they fell and making them appear suspended in air. Bart
Pierce was there, but he looked so tired that I didn't have the
heart to interview him. Though it was close to midnight, there
were still speakers lined up, waiting their turn. And as I
watched, someone was playing a guitar and singing. I was sur-

prised that he could play at all — with the wind, the chill factor must have brought the temperature down in the low forties.

It was with relief that, out of the corner of my eye, I noted Dean waving his arm. If we left now, we might get three hours' sleep before we had to get up again. But even more than that, I looked forward to a hot shower.

14

Like A Mighty Army

An alarm clock went off in the darkness, followed almost immediately by another in the next room, and then the telephone started ringing. Good grief, would there be an air-raid siren next? Muzzily my mind groped its way upwards to consciousness. It couldn't be four o'clock already! I had barely fallen asleep, my mind racing with stored-up dreams that my subconscious had had little opportunity to express during the past few nights. If I took the phone off the hook and turned my deaf ear up, my mind could plunge back down to delta level sleep in less than five minutes. . . .

But in the next room I could hear John up and moving about, and that meant we all would be, soon enough. Answering the phone as pleasantly as possible, I thanked the night clerk for the wake-up call and whispered, "Feet on floor!" It was a command which my body sullenly complied with. "Come on," I almost said aloud, "you'll feel better with a shave and your teeth brushed." I'll bet, my body replied. Groaning, we got up and shuffled to the bathroom, taking short steps and trying not to open our eyes more than slits. . . . While traveling in the Orient, my body had learned the art of staying asleep while appearing to be mobile. "Oh, come off it; you've never been to the Orient. Now brush those teeth!" One had to take a firm hand when the troops began to murmur. This was no time for an insurrection. Don't even look over at that inviting overstuffed chair!

When I had finished in the bathroom, Dean had still not budged. Aha, he had turned *his* deaf ear up! "C'mon, Dean," I mumbled without any enthusiasm, and then began to shuffle toward the chair.

Just then the door to the adjacent room opened. "Is everybody up?" asked John cheerily. "It's 4:15, and John and Dan will be in the lobby in fifteen minutes. Also, it's stopped raining," he announced, completing his report.

Dean bestirred himself, and I opened my eyes enough to look out the window. It was dark out (which should not have been surprising, since it was dark in). The sky was overcast (when had it ever been anything else?), and it looked once again as if it was about to rain. "Well," quipped John, "it would appear that the rain is about to fall on the just, as well as the unjust."

While Dean rumbled about in the bathroom, I dressed and double-checked my camera bag: recorder, back-up batteries, binoculars, telephoto lens, wide-angle, auto-winder, back-up batteries for that, and four different kinds of film for every possible condition — rolls and rolls of it.

I imagined a satellite view of Washington at that moment. In concentric circles ringing the city, hundreds of buses were poised to bring their pilgrims to the Mall, with the outermost ones, perhaps two hours away, already starting their engines. Soon they would all begin creeping towards the center, and a second wave would follow behind them, like an amphibious landing, bringing more and more and more Christians, until, like a mighty army, we had gathered, a hundred thousand strong — two hundred thousand — three. . . . I began to get excited. "Hey, Dean! Let's go!"

Dan and John were waiting for us when we got downstairs, and we started for the Mall. The sidewalks of Washington were not entirely deserted, even at that loneliest of hours. There were night people, some clutching bottles in brown paper bags, others poking desultorily through litter bins. And there were those like ourselves, sleepily drifting towards the Mall, to be there well before the opening prayer at six o'clock that morning.

A patrol car cruised by, and I looked at my watch: 4:45. This had to be the low-water mark of the evening, activity-wise. There wasn't another car in sight. I wondered what kind of a strain the rally would put on D.C.'s transportation system. They normally had a quarter of a million regular visitors on any given day. If that number were doubled, it probably wouldn't upset things too much. But if it were quintupled. . . . Still, I doubted that there was any real danger of "grid-lock," the spectre which haunted Manhattan's traffic control experts, whenever there was an unusually heavy influx of vehicles. Grid-lock occurred when all the city's cross streets were jammed so solid with cars that the uptown and downtown avenues jammed up as well. When that happened, a state of emergency was declared, and every available tow-truck was sent out on the sidewalks to start hauling out cars.

While we were still a few blocks from the Mall, John Sorensen left us, and headed for the Washington Monument. He wanted to get a tripod shot of the whole Mall from the top, while it was still dark, and then another at dawn — if there was a dawn. From where we were we could see the Monument with its pair of red aircraft warning lights; it seemed almost alive, brooding over the Mall with blinking red eyes.

The closer we got, the more anxious I became about how things were going to go during the day. I tried to remember what Jerry had said about God not bringing all of us so far, not to have His way there. But I could not help thinking of the frustrated Christian leaders who would like to give vent to their frustration. Lord *was* this day going to go Your way?

As if by way of an answer, we came up the sidewalk behind a middle-aged black woman, who was also headed in our direction. She wore an old blue parka, and did not hear us drawing near. As we approached, she stooped, picked up a piece of discarded paper and deposited it in a litter barrel on the corner. We passed her at that moment, and I noted that she was wearing a big Washington For Jesus button, and an equally big smile. I felt like hugging her. "Morning!" I exclaimed, with a grin.

"Yessir, brother, praise the Lord!" she replied, grinning back. I practically skipped down the street. Talk about God being in charge!

It was still pitch dark when we reached the Mall itself. We had to walk gingerly now to avoid the myriad forms huddled in damp sleeping bags, sometimes two or three side by side for warmth. They were everywhere — on benches and under them, on tarps on the ground, and a few far-sighted ones had brought back-packers' pup-tents. We four were all wide awake now, and a fresh wave of excitement swept through us, as we surveyed the incredible scene before us. Out of the darkness on all sides loomed shadowy forms, as more and more early comers arrived. Ahead, flanking the speakers' platform, were the towering silhouettes of the two sound scaffoldings. They were five stories high, with massive speakers pointed in every conceivable direction, to broadcast the spoken and sung word the length and breadth of the Mall, from the Monument clear to the Capitol. High above us in one of the towers, a work light formed a yellow halo in the night mist, as a sound technician raced against time, making final adjustments. These battlement-like silhouettes, coupled with the old Smithsonian castle in the middle, combined to give the effect of a stage setting for some Shakespearean tragedy. The whole backdrop was so imposing that it caused us to speak in whispers, though there was no one within earshot of a natural voice.

At the northern perimiter of the enclosure there was a group of a couple of thousand of those who were too wound up to sleep (they reminded me of my daughter having friends over for a slumber party — if anyone slumbered, it was a miracle.) They were singing old favorites, like "He is Lord," and "Amazing Grace," and they sang softly, so as not to disturb those still trying to sleep. There was a sweetness to that hushed singing, unlike anything I had heard. "Boy, am I glad I'm here!" I whispered to no one in particular.

"Me, too!" one of our group responded.

And Dan, who was perhaps the least easily impressed, murmured, "This is the most fantastic thing I've ever seen!"

We split up then, and I checked into the command center, to see what was happening and found Jerry and the others there, amazingly calm, though it was obvious that they had been up most, if not all, of the night. So, what was the latest word, this glorious morning?

"The latest word," said Jerry sardonically, "is that the police have just announced that anyone who does not have their car off of Jefferson or Madison within the next ten minutes is going to have it towed away." Even as he spoke, there was a muted rumble of engines outside; glancing out the window of the vehicle, I saw a squad of policemen on mopeds, riding down Jefferson.

But Jerry was uncharacteristically down about something, and when I asked him what it was, he showed me the morning paper's weather report: 100% chance of rain, winds gusting to 60 miles an hour, temperature not to get much above 60° (it was a clammy 52° now) — it sounded about as dismal a forecast as you could imagine. (A local cabbie had once told me that in D.C., a 30% chance of rain was a virtual assurance that sometime during the day you were going to get wet.) No wonder he was so glum!

I laughed, and when he asked why, I said, "Because it's going to make such a great story for the book, when God breaks the sun through!"

"I hope you're right," he smiled wanly, and inwardly I had to admit that my humor was mostly bravado.

I ducked back outside, too excited myself to stay put anywhere for very long. The sky was lightening rapidly now — there was a pink haze behind the seven bizarre towers of the old castle, none of which matched any of the others, and the flags at the back of the platform, dozens of them of all states and nations, flapped in the breeze. There were many more people present now, as six o'clock approached. Along the northern side of the Mall I could make out the huge state banners that people would march under in the parade, and it looked like many people were already gathering around their banners for the day. And coming down the walkways from the Monument end of the Mall, the trickle of people had become a steady stream. All told, I guessed there were some thirty thousand people, with their numbers increasing by a thousand a minute.

Thanks to the staff pass that Jerry had arranged for me, I was able to get up on the speakers' platform, and I did so now, at a quarter to six, for the best possible view. It was still very cold and raw, and I pulled my raincoat closer about me; you could see your breath on the air. Promptly at six, John Gimenez stepped to the clear plastic podium and said, "Let's pray." As he began, his manner was so informal and disarming that it felt like we were in someone's living room, praying with old friends — all thirty or forty thousand of us. He called on God to look down on us there and bless our undertaking and every single person who would come to the Mall during the day. And with that, Washington For Jesus had begun.

By 6:15, the sun would have been coming up behind the Capitol, but a heavy, dark overcast sat directly over Capitol Hill. The sky looked even more foreboding to the west, where the weather was coming from; in fact, we were ringed with foul weather. The only clear sky seemed to be directly overhead, turning blue now, rather than pink.

During that first hour, it seemed like some of the people who were most special to John spoke, though I knew that no conscious effort had been made to set it up that way. Nonetheless, sharing that most intimate hour of the long day were Violet Kiteley, David Schoch, Hispanic evangelist Raimundo Jiminez (speaking in Spanish, with an interpreter), Bishop Winley and Bill Wilson, another old-time Pentecostal pastor who had been behind John and his vision from the very beginning. Shortly before the end of that hour, Carlton Spencer, general chairman of Elim Fellowship, stepped to the podium and asked us to do something that I had never seen done at a charismatic rally: we each were to join with four or five of those around us in what was called *cluster prayer*. This we did, and as we were led in prayer, and then prayed ourselves in turn, we were knitted together in these little prayer groups, to the extent that many stayed together for fellowship for much of the day. This innovation from our evangelical brethren came as a surprise and a delight. It seemed that God was going to be showing us all something that day.

The second hour was a continuation of the first. Our ranks now swelled at the rate of two thousand a minute, and I circulated among them. The mood was very peaceful, very considerate, and also expectant. Around 8:30, I met Rob Gwynne from San Francisco and before that, Christ Church, New Zealand. It seemed that he had been keeping the folks down under informed of WFJ's progress, and a lot of churches throughout New Zealand were fasting and praying for America today. What was more, the Prime Minister's wife, a born-again Christian, was leading many people in prayer, and it seemed like there might even be a Wellington For Jesus next year.

Back at the speakers' platform, I had a chance to talk briefly with Vinson Synan, general secretary of the Pentecostal Holiness Church. What was his reaction so far? "To see this vast number of evangelicals willing to come together on the same platform with pentecostals and charismatics — it's a new dimension, an even greater dimension of unity than has been in this nation before. . . . Maybe all of the Christians are seeing that the forces of Satan are so united that we cannot afford any longer to stay divided as we have. We've got to join hands together. Today is one of the greatest demonstrations of unity that we have ever had in the history of this nation."

The next time I looked at my watch, it was 9:05, and Jim Bakker was speaking. He said, "Many people are saying America has one last chance. But I say, no, America's got one last *choice:* choose this day whom you will serve."

I wandered out in back of the speakers' platform and ran into John French, who told me that he had talked to one woman who had hung in at RFK stadium until the very end. She said that it was three o'clock when she finally left, and there were still several thousand people out there. She had taken the subway, and had been too excited to sleep. He also talked to a man who had come up on a special train from Jacksonville; it had left there Monday at 4:40 PM, and arrived here at 6:20 this morning, and more than 400 had come up that way. Finally, he was very pleased to see the way the WFJ staff was dealing with people who were attempting to pass out their own literature: anything that did not have Washington For Jesus on it was simply not permitted.

John and I both had our raincoats on, and we wondered if it was ever going to warm up. The sky above now was a solid grey overcast, with no blue in sight anywhere. It was a little after ten, and the rally was in high gear: these next two "prime time" hours would have the widest TV coverage of all, going "live" on the CBN and PTL networks, as well as on Trinity's cable TV satellite. I moved around in front of the speakers' platform, stepping carefully, for the mud here was a couple of inches deep. I stood, head bowed, as a black pastor from

Watts, Dr. E.V. Hill, led the assembly in prayer. "We believe that You're going to save us from the wrath that is sure to come unless we repent. We acknowledge our weaknesses and our wickedness. We acknowledge that we have strayed far from thee, but we know that thou art a loving God, thou art a merciful God, and so we say, in the name of the Lord Jesus, save us, Lord. Restore us, Lord. Bless us, Lord."

As he began to pray these last phrases, something made me look up, and to my amazement the overcast above seemed to be lightening. It couldn't be! But it was. Others noticed, and there was a murmur, even as Dr. Hill was concluding. And with the words, "Bless us, Lord," the cloud cover simply split and a shaft of pale sunlight fell on the gathering. A tremendous cheer went up, and the split widened. Next to me, a secular reporter from the Texas *Ledger* turned to his cameraman and said, shaking his head, "They're not going to *believe* this, when I file this copy!"

Now everyone was raising his hands to the sky, and the heavens parted still further, till the sun came through strong and clear, and that was the way it remained for the rest of the day. In the space of an hour, the temperature climbed twenty degrees, and it could not have been a more gorgeous day. Demos and others had been hoping that God would give a visible sign of His blessing on the rally; it seemed to me that He could not have given a more perfect or welcome one.

John Gimenez was speaking now, and I was able to catch the last part of what he was saying. He was sharing about how he had tried to talk himself out of the vision: "You're crazy, John; you're out of your head! This can't happen; there's too many divisions, too many separations of too much bitterness, too much criticism. You've got the white church, and you've got the black church, and you've got the Puerto Rican church, and you've got this church, and you've got that church — it can't happen; it's impossible! But somehow, I've learned that if we've turned to God, and God says get out of the boat, *then get out of the boat!* It's guaranteed that He'll solidify the water, and you'll walk on it. . . .''

Well, I thought, there John is, and here all of us are — God is truly Lord of the impossible!

At around eleven, I came across John Colbert, the head of the Mayor's Task Force. He was having a wonderful time, and I asked him for an official crowd estimate, for the people had been pouring in all morning long, and still were. He said that, as he had left the office an hour ago, the estimate was put at 200,000, which was what the mayor's office was telling the media. That would make it larger than the Pope's visit, he said, and in fact, larger than anythng since the Bi-Centennial celebration. I said that it seemed to me that the crowd was at least a quarter larger than it had been an hour earlier, which would make it 250,000, and he agreed.

Looking around now from up on the speakers' platform with the sun out, there was a whole different mood on the Mall now. People had taken their coats off, and some of the grass was already dry enough to sit on — the entire atmosphere was like a church picnic without the food.

I was standing near Paul Crouch, the head of Trinity Broadcasting, who was wearing a white suit that seemed almost iridescent in the sun. How did he feel about the way the rally was going? ''I feel this is the beginning of the revival that God has promised to pour out on our nation and our world. We'll just have to follow through with it now and really take the spirit and the electricity that we feel in this place today back to our homes, our television stations, our churches, and really cooperate with the Holy Spirit and go out into the highways and byways, compelling people to come in.''

At the microphone, the speaker was Adrian Rogers, president of the Southern Baptist Convention whose thirteen million members made it the largest denomination in the country. I caught one thing he said (which was also picked up by AP and was quoted in papers all across the country): *''America, once the mightiest of nations, has become the laughingstock of the nations. The scream of the American eagle has become the twitter of a frightened sparrow.''*

I had never heard it summed up quite so succinctly. I glanced at my watch — it was almost noon. The parade would be starting in a few minutes. I left the speakers' platform and went around behind it, where who should be strolling down Jefferson Drive but the sixteenth President, complete with full-length black coat and tall hat and beard. As Fritz Klein, made up as Lincoln, went through the checkpoint at the gate, the security man in charge leaned over to him and said: ''Don't worry, Mr. President, we've got our eye on Booth.''

Just then, Dean came up and with him was Sam Cherney, the head of the security force. I told them what I had just overheard, and they laughed. We talked about the security problems, of which there had been remarkably few. Sam said that there were several groups of dissidents on the fringes, but his men had them under surveillance, and thus far there had been no trouble of any sort.

What sort of an assignment had it been? ''Security is 80% planning and 20% execution. And of course, we've never seen anything quite this size before, so there are variables that we can't predict. It's planning for them and developing a contingency plan that's been the greatest difficulty we've had.''

How was it to work with the Metropolitan Police? ''The Metropolitan Police and Park Police have given us great assistance. They're such professionals at handling crowds of this size that they've been tremendous. It's had an effect on them, too. I mean, there's no crowd antagonism. They've never seen such a positive group of people.''

Speaking of the group and the few dissident elements, like a handful of militant homosexuals, and a cadre from the Children of God, and the shoeless blanket people that I had seen the other morning, the security agents had noted a truly extraordinary thing: whenever these dissident elements would approach the speakers' enclosure, perhaps with the intent of creating a disruption, the people in front of them seemed to shift and close ranks, without even being aware that they were doing so. And not only were the dissidents blocked, but as they tried to force their way forward, they were gradually worked back out to the periphery. It was as if a body was instinctively rejecting a foreign substance. Which it was.

It was noon, and I hurried out to Jefferson Drive. The parade was just getting under way, and I wanted to get a shot of that, as they swung down Constitution Avenue.

James Kennedy, David DuPlessis and John Mears

n and Viola Malachuk

Adrian Rogers and John Hall

Vonette Bright

Fr. John Randall

In Congressman Rhodes' office

Demos Shakarian

Fr. John Bertolucci

Tammy Bakker

and Shirley

Ben Kinchlow

Jim Bakker and Paul Crouch

Vo

Ben Haden

and John

en Black, Kansas City, Mo.

Pat and Jim

John and Anne

"Glory, Glory, Hallelujah!"

Hometown band makes good!

Even the atheists were represented — and loved!

15

"For Thine is the Glory"

Captain Mazur's men had cleared Jefferson Drive down to 7th Street, and the captain turned and scowled, to see what was holding up the leaders of the parade. It was a mob of photographers and well-wishers and autograph-seekers that had come from out of nowhere and swarmed around the three chairmen and their wives, and Arthur Blessit and his cross. But soon things got underway, with the Brights and the Robertsons linking arms with Arthur, and moving out at a good pace.

As they swung onto Constitution Avenue, a large crowd was gathered at the corner. Cheering broke out, and people waved flags and banners; there was as much excitement as a ticker-tape parade for a returning hero. Someone in the vanguard started singing, "Mine eyes have seen the glory of the coming of the Lord;" it caught on and was to become the theme song for the entire march.

Along with several other photographers, I ran backwards in front of them, pausing to kneel and shoot this historic occasion, and then falling back again, to repeat the process. I began to feel a little like a minute man in front of the British on the road to Concord. Having shot all the film in my camera, I asked Pat how it felt to be marching down the center of Washington, flanked by a dozen Christians on either side, with a hundred thousand more behind him.

"Well, it's like a dream," he said, above all the cheers and the singing. "I can't believe it's happening, and yet it's happening before our eyes. The greatest crowd every assembled to the glory of God in this nation's capital — there's never been anything like it! And to see the willingness of people to give their lives to Christ — it's awesome!"

I turned to Arthur: was the cross getting heavy?

"No, you know, Jesus bore our sins, and it's a joy and privilege and blessing to be able to carry the cross and remind people that it's not so heavy. *He* bore the heavy weight."

In no time at all, it seemed that we were turning left up 14th Street, where the marchers would then turn back onto the Mall and disperse. Two cars with security agents suddenly pulled up, whisked the leaders into them, and roared off, almost before we knew what was happening. Everyone else could relax and have a good time but the men charged with the responsibility for the principals' safety.

I headed back up the parade route, reloading my camera more by feel than anything else. Here came the Cops for Christ, with their lovely white banner, and following them were the Alabama and Alaska contingents. The latter were carrying many well-lettered placards, including JUNEAU FOR JESUS and GOD'S CHOSEN FROZEN. And then came Arizona, the state that I seemed to have adopted as a model for the book. There was Derald McDaniel, the state coordinator, at the head of their group; what was he thinking about, at that moment?

He shook his head. "It's unbelievable! There's no way to express this. We were just saying, there's no way to describe this, when we go back home. It's just unbelievable!"

Arkansas came next, and then an enormous contingent from

California. The march organizers had hoped to limit the number from each state to a thousand, but how could you tell someone who had driven or flown all the way from California that they couldn't march? By the time I had passed them, and they passed me, I was almost back up to 7th Street. But then, instead of Colorado, who should come down the avenue but Canada For Jesus! I couldn't believe it: here were Doug Burke, Geoffrey Shaw, Paul Weigle and a whole bunch of friends from "100 Huntley Street" Christian television program, whom I hadn't seen since I finished working on David Mainse's book.

"Hey, Doug, how about Ottawa For Jesus next summer?"

"Amen!" he shouted, laughing.

I walked with the forty or so Canadians visiting, and then started back towards 7th Street again. As Colorado came by, I noticed a bearded old man carrying a large placard and wearing denim pants and jacket all covered with buttons. A closer look revealed him to be a one-man representative of the Virginia chapter of the American Atheists. His placard was covered with bumper stickers that said things like "In Reason We Trust" and "I never needed it!" and in the middle of his back was a huge button with the face of Madalyn Murray O'Hair. I took a photo of him, and as I was about to turn away, a woman detached herself from the Colorado contingent and came over and gave him a great big hug.

In Colorado, I knew exactly one Christian brother, Mel Berg, and his was the very next face I clapped eyes on. (Was this happening to everyone? Running into so many friends from so far apart?) I told Mel about the scene I'd just witnessed and asked him what he thought of the size of the crowd. "You know," he said wryly, "there's been so many people who thought that they really wouldn't have the crowds," he added, peering about, "but everybody's here. Looks to me like nobody's missing."

I said goodbye and ducked across the street in front of Connecticut, to join the parade-watchers who were sitting packed together on the steps of the Archives Building. It felt awfully good to sit down for a moment, and I realized that I'd been on my feet without a break for nine hours, the last hour walking backward, for the most part, along the parade route.

I rested until Iowa, then got up and again headed back toward 7th Street. I had just about gotten to the corner when along came Kansas, and there in the lead was another old friend, Warren Black. It turned out he was state coordinator, and his response to the march was no less than I'd come to expect. "I tell you, David, this is the highlight of my life — a wonderful, wonderful gathering!"

Finally, I got to 7th Street just in time to see our community band step off the curb and into position in the ranks of the Massachusetts contingent. As they turned down Constitution Avenue and struck up "The Stars and Stripes Forever," I noticed a grin pass from policeman to policeman, like dominoes, as they stood at parade rest, every thirty feet along the route. I asked one what he thought of the march so far. "It's one of the two best parades I've seen in the past five years." What was the other one? "The Pope's motorcade." What did he think about the attitude of this one? "I've never seen so many happy people! I mean, it's great; I wish they could have routed it further."

I hadn't seen John Sorensen all day, but I knew that he must have gotten some good shots from the top of the Monument. All at once, I had a strong desire to see what the Mall looked like from there myself, and so, completing the parade route for about the third time, I went up the knoll, and then up the elevator. At the top, a cool breeze blew in through the small open window, at which one of the WFJ cameras was positioned, its zoom lens focused on the parade. I got out my binoculars and surveyed the Mall. There was still a tremendous crowd there, but I noted that there was green grass visible both to the east and west of the main mass of people around the enclosure. There was vacant ground, especially towards 7th Street, which probably meant that the former occupants were either marching, or had left the Mall entirely, to get some lunch. Even so, it was a good deal fuller than it had been at ten, when they put the figure at 200,000. Looking down at the scene, it was hard to find anything to compare it to. Only once had I ever seen so many people in one place before, and that was in St. Peter's square in Rome, when John Paul I made his next to last public appearance. There were simply people everywhere, like that Atlanta railroad yard scene from "Gone with the Wind," only these couldn't have been happier. There was something else, too: the sound system was doing its job. Jerry needn't have worried; you could hear the speakers all the way up here, and they were coming *against* the wind! There was no echo either, unlike some places on the Mall, where you could hear a triple echo, as the sound bounced from granite building to granite building.

On my way back to the Mall, I asked Captain Layfield, the officer in charge of the motorcycle police, for a comment. "Well, I've seen a lot of parades in this town; these people are different than most." How did he mean? "Well, I think that they're Christians, and that makes the whole difference." How? "You know," he said, a bit impatiently, "they're looking out after each other. They're not trying to run each other down. They're acting the way they all should."

I went back to the command center (partly because they had comfortable seats), and found Carol Owen in a traditional pose, with a phone cradled on her shoulder. How was the operations plan working out? "Beautifully," she said, hanging up the phone. "Of course, nothing is working out the way we planned. There were so many more people than we expected arriving to park at RFK this morning, that the subway couldn't handle them all. We just completely overloaded their circuits. But we had 167 buses held in reserve to bring people in from out-of-town parking lots, and so we mobilized these and pressed them into service to get people here from RFK, so it's all working out.''

At that point, Bart Pierce and Jerry Kantowski returned from the 1:15 press conference, and from the look on their faces, it had not gone well.

"It was murderous," Jerry said. "They were so vicious, you wouldn't have believed it, and finally Ronn Kerr just said, 'That's it; no more questions.' Their questions weren't making any sense; they were just filled with hatred, saying that the grass-roots people were sincere, 'but you rotten guys in leadership, you're the ones!' But the three co-chairmen just kept going back to God: 'We're here to pray.' ''

It sounded to me like once again, Satan had completely blown his cool and was lashing out at the thing he hated that was happening on the Mall.

"As we were leaving," Jerry added, "the most hostile of them screamed a name at Bill Bright, and John took him by the shoulder and quietly said, 'Now you wait a minute.' Right away, secret service guys intervened and said, 'Come on, let's get out of here,' and hustled us all away.''

On the other hand, Bart could not have been more exuberant about how things had gone out at RFK the night before. ''The way those artists kept right on playing in the rain was a testimony in itself. We saw them standing there with the make-up running down their faces, and their hair gone flat, and they just kept ministering unto the Lord. Barry McGuire was so touched, he was weeping the whole time before he went out on the platform, and artists would kneel down in the water, and God just poured out His grace on them, and three of the local work crew got saved. And "Truth" played with "Candle" and the "Imperials" played with "Truth," and they all got together, worshipping the Lord and saying, 'No, you go on.' I tell you, man it *happened!"*

He remembered something else: "The stadium people called me this morning and said we left the stadium perfect!"

Anne Gimenez came by then, and I asked her what had been her reaction during the parade. "As we came along, people applauded and waved and lifted their hands and pointed one finger up — they welcomed and blessed and worshipped with us. In the whole march, there was not any animosity — somewhere else there might have been, but not during the march."

And then John Gilman stopped in. I asked him if he had a minute or two, since he had been so busy attending to the speakers' schedule that he'd had scarcely time to slow to a walk. That schedule had gone remarkably well, all things considered. Practically everyone had been faithful to the time allotted them, until early in the afternoon when one evangelist, perhaps overcome at the prospect of addressing such a multitude, had gone on and on and on, ignoring the cue cards which were held up in front of him. Even so, after nine hours, they were running only twenty minutes or so behind.

John and I walked outside and away from the command center. He looked over at the little carousel in the distance and said, "I think the thing that scares me, that I'm concerned about, is symbolized by that circus tent over there. We could dissipate our energy or lose our direction here. We have the ability at this point to turn this into a circus, and what was born in hardship and all these men like Francis and Jerry and tremendous lists of people who have poured out their blood, sweat and tears, and prayed every day — their efforts would be for nothing. The only thing that will save it is if we continue this brokenness and being humbled before God."

He looked out at all the people on the Mall. "I think if the leadership that's here will unite to emphasize humility and continuing humbleness before God, that we won't have to worry about the outcome of this rally. But if we think we've won a great victory by just being here today, we've missed the whole point of God's eternal plan, which is that we become a holy people, always.''

And then he said something startling: "We had a bomb threat, you know, behind the platform here. It was reported in the Smithsonian and needed to be checked out. They cleared the back area, and though it turned out to be a false alarm, I'll tell you, you get humble real quick, when it looks like you might be about to go to the Lord.''

Just then Bill Bright's assistant, John Jones, who was functioning as John Gilman's counterpart among the evangelicals, came up to check something with him. What did he think of how the scheduling was going? "It's remarkably well disciplined, and I think it exhibits the Lord's blessing very much. I feel like God has really been guiding and helping us.''

The speaker on the platform now was Ben Haden, and we stopped to listen. "We don't have a license to sin; we have a license to *obey*. Let us so live in this nation that God will look upon this nation and forgive this nation because of the believers. The United States is never coming to repentance. The *believers* must come to repentance, and for our repentance alone, our Lord will respond.''

Several people said amen to that, and he went on: "For my own part, I repent, and point the finger at no one but myself . . . . O Lord, may we here, beginning today, in the privacy of our own lives, and in the way we live publicly and advertize Jesus Christ — may we with godly sorrow repent of the way we've been living, of the things we've been serving, of the things that unconsciously we have worshipped, and remember that we have one God. O Lord, bless us with an awareness of the oneness of the Godhead and the only-ness of our Christ. In thy name we praise thee, Amen.''

I went up on the speakers' platform and noted that at 3:45, we had reached the highwater mark, as far as attendance was concerned. The Mall was packed solid from 7th Street to 14th Street; there wasn't a big of green grass to be seen anywhere. David DuPlessis was waiting to speak. He had just flown in from Oslo, and his travels recently had been taking him all over the globe. "When you think of the millions who are watching on television," he said, "nothing that I've seen lately could make a bigger impact on America than this. In fact, on the world — for the world doesn't think that such a meeting is possible in America. I think that it's possible *only* here, for I know of no other capital in the world that would allow half a million people to gather on their lawns like this and set up all this plant here for Christ. They would say, well, this church won't like it, and that church won't like it, and the Moslems won't like it. But our government is still Christian enough to allow Christ to be honored and prayer to be said."

Just leaving the platform was Jim Bakker, the head of PTL. Now that the afternoon was drawing to a close, what effect did he think the rally was going to have on Washington? "I'm sure it's going to have a profound effect upon Senators and Congressmen and even on the White House, that they're going to have to realize there's a lot of Christians out there that want a nation under God." And what about the impact on the people watching at home? "When you consider that all three of our networks are carrying this live right now, and I know that we will be putting excerpts into our prime program during the next few days, multiplied millions will be here via television, so it is probably the largest single event in the history of Christianity." Was he glad to be a part of it? "Yes! It's part of the coming of the Lord, part of the fulfillment of prophecy, the Word of God. It's a real signal that Jesus is coming soon. The Church knows it, you can tell — you can feel it!"

As Jim left, Paul Crouch, Trinity Broadcasting Network's

chief, was speaking. He said that if you held out your hand, you might feel an invisible miracle happening. From three satellites, there was live television coverage of that moment, pouring down on America, from Honolulu to Washington.

I turned to Fr. John Bertolucci, who was soon to speak, and asked him what was on his heart. "Just sitting here, I look to my left and I see the famous memorial . . . and here we are, surrounded by buildings built by men which are symbolic of our government, symbolic of humanity, and all this is good, but Jesus Christ is the greater power . . . . It's only through Christ Power, through Spirit Power, through the power of the united Body of Christ, that this nation will be saved from the precipice of disaster . . . . Jesus makes the difference. He is the answer, and this Christ Power is what the world has been looking for: no other political power, no other ideological power, no other philosophical power can change the course of history . . . . In Revelation, He says, 'See, already I am making all things new,' and this is what the Lord is doing by gathering this assembly. This *is* a gathering of the Lord, and with it He *is* already making things new."

Time was passing quickly now; it was almost 5:00, and the shadows were beginning to elongate and stretch towards the Capitol. The sun was still out, but it had gotten a little cooler. I had a chance to visit with Ben Haden just before he left, and it seemed to both of us that the spirit of unity was stronger now than it had ever been; in fact, it had been building all afternoon. "I've never seen as much prayer answered," he said. "There's unity here that I've never known since I was a believer."

Out in back of the speakers' platform, I found Jim Rubin who was in charge of the National Park Service people who were responsible for the Mall. Jim was an old hand at estimating crowds; how many people would he say were here now? "Based on comparative crowds, I would say you had at least

300,000 here, counting those who are always on the move, behind us. There's a lot of people on Independence Avenue and a lot in the museums, so I wouldn't feel at all uncomfortable with 300,000.''

Would he go to 350,000? No, he smiled and shook his head.

But there was green grass showing now, a lot of it, especially on the 7th Street side. If there were 300,000 now, that meant that there were *at least* 350,000 at 3:45. And if you figured that by that late in the afternoon, 150,000 of those who had come early in the morning had already left, in order to beat the rush hour, then half a million would be a conservative estimate.* It was less than the million that had been hoped for, as the media were already pointing out in the afternoon news (using the mayor's office 10:00 AM estimate of 200,000), but it was still more people gathered for one event, other than the Bi-Centennial, than the nation had ever seen.

The last person I talked to was Bill Bright. The security man assigned to him had just shared with him that after Bill had prayed for him, another Christian had led him to the Lord, and Bill was obviously touched. When I asked him if he had an explanation for the increasing sense of unity that was present, he chuckled. ''We've had a chance to hear each other preach — the charismatics, the non-charismatics, the Baptists, the Catholics, the Methodists, and all, and so now we're beginning to say: Look, we are members of the same family; we can worship God together. This day is God's, and I believe that from this day forward, God is going to do new things, and we're going to see revival such as we've never seen before in the history of the nation.''

A few minutes past six, the program was over. People were leaving the Mall in all directions, and as they left, I watched them look around and pick up any pieces of paper near them, so that the green grass was left spotless, cleaner even than it had been the day before, when it was empty.

John Gimenez was at the microphone. ''We want to do one

more thing before we go. We want to join together our hands, our hearts and our spirits, and we want to sing the Lord's Prayer. Those of you on the way out there, would you stop a moment and join hands?'' And all of those about to leave turned and did so, making a chain of believers that wound back and forth, as more and more linked up.

"As we hold hands,'' continued John, "let's keep in our hearts and minds the prayer of our Lord Jesus: *that we might be one.* As we sing the Lord's Prayer, could you really just put it in your heart that we're going home to work for *unity* in the Church of Jesus Christ? We'll have differences, but we'll have unity.''

John Hall led the singing, and the well-known words pronounced a benediction over the Mall — and the city. "For Thine is the kingdom and the power and the glory — '' All hands went up, and the setting sun, which had been behind a cloud, now shone across the Mall, from directly behind the peak of the Washington Monument.

As the last "Amen'' died away, John said, "Don't let this be the end. Let it be the beginning of the unity of the Church of the Lord Jesus Christ.''

* We later received unexpected confirmation of this figure from an unorthodox but highly credible source: Ron Boehme reported that his Youth With A Mission volunteers handed out 482,000 WFJ newspapers on the Mall. They gave them out only to adults, and only one to a customer. Many people turned them down, having already picked up their copies the night before, and as diligent as YWAM teams were, they felt that they had not been able to reach everyone. Therefore, though we later heard of semi-official estimates as high as 750,000, as far as we were concerned, half a million was realistic.

16

Going Home

At dinner that evening, there was a nostalgic wistfulness at the table, almost as if we were sorry that it was all over. Each of us had been stretched to the limit, and had lived there for several days, none of us getting more than four hours' sleep a night and usually less. In the morning, the others would be leaving, while Dean and I stayed in town for a couple of days, tying up loose ends, but we all felt like combat soldiers who had grown close under fire, and were now being mustered out.

I asked each one, in turn, if anything memorable had happened to them. For Dean, one of the things was meeting David DuPlessis again, after three years. Out in Kansas City, we had given him a lift to the airport, and Dean had suddenly been led to contribute the contents of his wallet to David's ministry, something he had never done before. This afternoon, he had done the same thing again.

John French couldn't get over how decent the people had been — thoughtful, considerate and well-behaved. They were not just middle America, John said, they were the very best of middle America, the finest example of the sort of Americans this country could produce.

John Sorensen told about a Washington *Star* photographer

that he had befriended in the rain, out at RFK. The man was not a Christian, but when he came to the end of his roll and needed a dry place to change film, John invited him under the umbrella he had brought to protect his tripod and telephoto lens. They got to talking, and John ran into him again several times during the rally. He had a chance to witness to him, and it seemed to him that the man's attitude grew steadily more open.

I told about a free-lance house-painter I had talked to after the parade, who had lost a $1500 job because he felt that he was supposed to come to the rally and march in the parade. He was concerned about it, because he had also displeased the house-builder who usually sub-contracted to him. But while he was here, of all things, he was talking to a couple who had bought a large, old house two hours from where he lived and who wanted the whole thing painted. They asked the house-painter if he would do it, and from the size of the house, the job was going to run just about $1500!

But it was Dan Ford who surprised us all. When it came to people and emotions and motivations, Dan, who was a top salesman and past president of the fastest-growing industrial real estate firm in the midwest, was a born skeptic. "I thought many times that where I was at a few years ago, I could have been standing in exactly the same spot as I was in today, hearing what I heard, and I would have been completely turned off by everything. My reaction would have been: why don't these people stop pontificating, the whole thing is ridiculous. But I realized today how much of a change the Lord had made in me, because as I listened to John Gimenez this morning, I broke into tears. It was Jesus that I saw in him, and I was just overcome — at the whole thing, all the people . . . " and he had to stop, because he was weeping again.

John Sorensen said, "Tell them about your tripod," and Dan, grateful for the interruption, did.

"Well, I was walking through the people, looking for good

shots, and I left the tripod up against a tree, and sort of forgot about it. I was so busy taking pictures that I wandered off and then couldn't remember where I'd left it.''

"What did it cost?'' someone said.

"Over a hundred dollars. But for some reason, I didn't have any great concern about it. I just went on shooting and walking, and a couple of hours later, I wandered back into the general area, and all of a sudden, there it was, right where I'd left it. The point is, I had a strong feeling I could have left it there all day, and nobody would have bothered it. That was the kind of people they were. I couldn't get over how peaceful everyone was, all day long. And you know, there really weren't that many scruffy-looking types at all, you know, with the scraggly hair and the dirty clothes and sandals, and all. In fact, a newspaper photographer who was trying to find a weirdo to photograph would have had a hard time.''

It was a quiet, peaceful evening, and I wondered if there wasn't the same sort of mood on all the hundreds of buses that were now heading away from Washington, like ever-widening ripples across the pond of America. We didn't stay up late, as I feared we might, and slept like logs, which was not too surprising.

In the morning, I had to call John Jones about something at 7:00, and promptly at 7:00, the wake-up call came. I felt like I had been run over by a truck. Every muscle in my body ached, and my bones felt like they had been dislocated. I called John, and had to smile when he answered: he sounded like he had been run over by a truck.

Where we were staying, there was a sauna and a steam room downstairs, so while Dean still slept, I made my way down there. When I came out, instead of feeling like a broken reed, I felt like a rubbery, broken reed. Well, breakfast would fix that, I said to myself, but it didn't. I felt like a rubbery, broken reed with a lead weight in its stomach. Later that morning, as Dean and John and I tried to do some business before John had to leave, I kept falling asleep in the middle of the conference.

I pulled myself together enough to accompany John, as he went over to the hotel where Arizona state coordinator Derald McDaniel was staying, as they were going to the airport together. I wanted to get Derald's post-impressions, to wrap up Arizona, and so creaked along, as John went chipperly up the sidewalk. When we got there, I asked Derald what the highpoint of the whole experience had been for him, expecting him to say the parade.

"I think the highpoint for me was Monday night. The atmosphere in that leaders' meeting was just electric. I've never felt anything like it. Another thing: to walk back and forth through that crowd on the Mall, which we did a number of times with people as far in both directions as you could see — it was just incredible."

What struck him the most about it?

"I think it was the orderliness — the quiet and the peace and the calm and the order — some people praying, some people reading, some people sleeping, and some standing and listening. The highpoint of that was around 5:00 yesterday, when we all turned and raised our hands toward the Capitol Building. Remember when we took spiritual authority over the strong man and bound him? That had a tremendous impact on Marilyn and me."

What did he think of the program?

"It was just sensational! I don't think there's anyway that you could improve on the format. The continuity was tremendous, and while we knew that people had been given assignments to speak on, still the Holy Spirit was tying it all together underneath."

Anything else? "Well, there was a sense of belonging — a sense of the family being together in that kind of setting. Like we were a family reunion and enjoying being there."

John asked Derald about the 40-hour prayer vigil for the rally that they had asked other Arizona churches to participate in. "I heard from more than a dozen pastors, who said that their people would be signing up for hours."

How had it gone with the delegations? "Excellent. From a spiritual point of view, the visit to Senator DeConcini was the highlight, because he really seemed attuned with our understanding of the need of spiritual emphasis. But all of them — all four of our Congressmen and our two Senators — were very happy to join hands with us and to have us pray for them and with them."

I said goodbye to John and Derald then, and made my way back to our room. Dean had gotten the morning's papers and read me the stories, which were lukewarm and downplayed at best. But thanks to John French and Luce Press Clippings, Inc. in New York, we had been getting clippings of all the WFJ coverage in the country, as well as transcripts of radio and TV coverage. Thus far it had been much lighter than we had expected, but we chalked that up to the aborted rescue attempt story, which was still pre-empting page one.

(The final count of media representatives who had registered to cover the rally was around 600 — more than had ever covered a religious event before. And in subsequent days, newspaper clippings that would fill several bushel baskets came in from all across America, including many letters to the editor from people who were there, and descriptions of some twenty rallies that went on simultaneously in other cities, in support of Washington For Jesus, unbeknownst to us. The wire services had done a good job, and several of the major dailies in the country had featured it. But the TV coverage was perfunctory at best, and there was no coverage whatsoever in the newsweeklies. That was ironic, considering that shortly before, 20,000 people marching for E.R.A. in Chicago had received a full page in *Time* and extensive TV coverage — ironic but not surprising, considering the number of editorial desks held by idealists who had little use for the doings of evangelical Christianity. By downplaying or simply ignoring the rally, they, in effect, turned it into a non-event in many influential areas of the secular media.)

I called Ted Pantaleo to check on a couple of things, and we got to talking about the coverage. He laughed. "Try to get a copy of the Baltimore *Sun,*" he said. "My mother just called, and she doesn't usually get excited about a thing like this, but it just knocked her out. The *Sun* came out with front-page coverage which referred, among other things specifically to the press conference yesterday afternoon. It said: 'Reverends John Gimenez, Pat Robertson and Bill Bright maintained their smiles and composure in the face of being attacked by a hostile Washington press.' That's pretty unusual for one respected major daily to say about another."

I agreed, and spent the rest of the day waiting for my body to recover. (Had others felt like they had lost a fight with a mule?) But as we left the next day, I felt well enough to suggest one last swing by the Mall. The platform was gone, the chain-link fence was gone — in fact, the only evidence of the rally was the trampled area in front of the Smithsonian, and that, too, would soon be gone.

As we drove slowly up Jefferson with the windows open, I said to Dean, "Stop here a moment." As we listened, we could just make out the wheezing sound of the old nickelodeon. I pointed out the little carousel and told Dean some of the things that had come to me, two weeks before.

"You know," he said, "I wonder if the Christians in this country are going to get off the merry-go-round now and start marching together. Or are we just going to keep going round and round, like we always have been?" He started up the car, and I, too, wondered if Washington For Jesus was going to be an end — or a beginning.

Epilogue

That fall, Dean and I were again in the car, this time driving John Gimenez and Jerry Kantowski over to the Rock Church. Washington For Jesus was past, but America For Jesus was very much in the future, with major rallies in twenty of the largest cities in America and a whole host of smaller ones. Each of these rallies would be carefully pre-planned and coordinated to culminate with a return to the Mall on April 29, 1982.

Dean and I were in Norfolk in connection with the initial planning meetings that would launch America For Jesus, for which coordinators had gathered from all across the country. As we rode, the sun was just rising over the Tidewater, and the subject of Jesse Winley came up. "You know," said John, "no death has ever affected me the way his did. When I got the call, I wept and in grief threw the phone away from me." He shook his head. "And I had even had a dream the night before, in which the Lord had told me that Jesse was dead, so that early morning call was merely confirmation." He paused. "I just didn't want to accept it."

He told us that the day before that call, he had received another. This one had come at 6:00 AM, and it was from the bishop himself. He had called John often enough before, to encourage him when he needed it most, but never had he called this early. "John," he said, "God told me to call you, because I'm going into the hospital this morning, and I may not make our next meeting in California. He gave me three words for you: first, you are not to *relinquish*. He has entrusted you with the vision, and if you relinquish control of it, now that it is a success, there are others who would eagerly take it over and use it for themselves. You must retain the authority!

"Second, you are to *pursue*. God has given the Church the victory; the enemy was taken by surprise and is off-balance. Now is not the time to quit the battlefield; now is the time to pursue, with equal vigor!

"Third, you are to *go out*. You are to go to Chicago, to New York, to San Francisco, and beyond. You are to raise up an army in the cities and the countryside and carry the message to the whole world!"

The bishop had one last thing to say: "Don't put your hope in political solutions; you'll only be disappointed. No candidate or party is capable of turning America around now, no matter how much they might promise to do so; things have gone too far. This is spiritual war, and Christ is now the only hope for America. But His Body must be united — to repent, to pray and to stand. Washington For Jesus was the beginning, but only the beginning."

John had remembered the words, but he had refused to accept their possible significance; Jesse had meant too much to him to think of losing him now. Then came the call, and later, as he went for a run down the beach and looked through his tears out at the Atlantic, God ministered to him in the midst of his grief. He reminded John of the riddle of Samson — *from out of the carcass came honey*. Jesse Winley had died, but his spirit that had been so close to the heart of Washington For Jesus would go on.

We drove along in silence, looking out at the pockets of ground fog being burned off my the morning sun. I recalled a similar reaction I had had at the sudden death of John Paul I, the "barefoot Pope" who had captured the hearts of hundreds of millions the world over. I could not understand why God had taken him so soon after elevating him. What came to me was that, as a reward for a lifetime of obedient service, in which he had truly manifested the spirit of Christ, God had given him as a crown that brief period as Pope. Similarly, at the end of Bishop Winley's lifetime of service, God had given him Washington For Jesus as his last assignment, and as a crown, the unparalleled reception that his preaching had received.

I shared this with the others, and Dean commented that this was once a tradition in the military — when a colonel had served well for thirty years or more, they would honor him by making him a general just before he retired. Perhaps it was not all that different in Christ's army. I chuckled, recalling the way Bishop Winley would glare at his audience and growl: "Brothers and sisters, this is *war!*"

And it *was* war — a spiritual battle was now being waged for the destiny of America. The Church was awakening, the call was going out. And doing their part was the headquarters staff of America For Jesus. Seasoned veterans now, they bore little resemblance to the ragged militia who had first answered the call two years ago. Gimenez, Gilman, Pantaleo, Kantowski, Owen, Pierce, Singleton, Cucuzza — their names even sounded like platoon roll in a World War II movie. But they had become tough and proficient soldiers, and the difference reminded me of what had happened to the Continental Army in the winter of Valley Forge. They had lost a third of their number, but they had been tempered, hardened and annealed, and when they emerged in the spring to pursue the British, they were, man for man, the best fighting troops in the world, as their red-coated adversaries were soon shocked to discover. God had done something similar during Washington For Jesus; the headquarters staff was still totally dependent upon His grace, and they knew it, but now they were a smoothly efficient, combat-tested team.

I suddenly recalled a dream which Jim Cucuzza had shared with me, driving me to the airport on my previous trip to Virginia Beach. It was one of those just-before-waking dreams that seem to be given then so that we'll be sure to remember them. In it, Jim was following three other men up a snow-covered hillside. He and the men in front of him were wearing tri-cornered hats, blue coats with cream-colored waistcoats and breeches, and shoes with silver buckles on them. The man in the lead was carrying an American flag, and a voice said to Jim: *This is your Valley Forge.*

That was all there was to the dream, and at the time, I could see no particular significance to it. But now the significance brought goose-bumps to my flesh. The army of the Lord was on the march and in pursuit!

*For he hath looked down from the height of his sanctuary;
from heaven did the Lord behold the earth . . . .
When the people are gathered together,
and the kingdoms, to serve the Lord.*

— *Psalm 102:19,22*

CHAIRMAN, NATIONAL STEERING COMMITTEE

Rev. John Gimenez
Pastor, Rock Church
Virginia Beach, Virginia

PROGRAM CO-CHAIRMEN

Dr. Bill Bright
Founder and President
Campus Crusade for Christ International

Dr. Pat Robertson
Founder and President
The Christian Broadcasting Network

Dr. Ben Armstrong
Executive Director
National Religious Broadcasters
Jim Bakker
President
PTL Television Network
Rt. Rev. Archimandrite Stephen Barham
Eastern Orthodox Church
Richardson, Texas
John Beckett
President
Intercessors of America
Dr. B. Clayton Bell
Pastor, Highland Park Pres. Church
Dallas, Texas
Dr. Eugene Bertermann
Long Time Former
President of NRB
Father John Bertolucci
Pastor, St. Joseph's Catholic Church
Little Falls, New York
Arthur Blessit
Author, Evangelist
Los Angeles, California
Pat Boone
Entertainer
Beverly Hills, California
Dr. Herbert Bowdoin
United Methodist Hour
Orlando, Florida
Rev. Harald Bredesen
Charisma Ministries
Escondido, California

Rev. Steve Brown
Key Biscayne Presbyterian Church
Key Biscayne, Florida
Martin M. Chernoff
Congregation Besh Yeshua
Jack Cohen
Executive Vice President
Greyhound Internatinal
Paul Crouch
President
Trinity Broadcasting Network
Nicky Cruz
Nicky Cruz Outreach
Colorado Springs, Colorado
Dr. Jimmy Draper
Pastor, First Baptist Church
Euless, Texas
David Du Plessis
"Mr. Pentecost"
Dr. Buckner Fanning
Pastor, Trinity Baptist Church
San Antonio, Texas
John Gilman
President
Dayspring Enterprises International
Ben Haden
Speaker, Changed Lives TV-Radio
Chattanooga, Tennessee
Jack Hayford
Pastor, Church on the Way
Van Nuys, California
Dr. E.V. Hill
Pastor, Mt. Zion Missionary Baptist Church
Los Angeles, California
Rex Humbard
Founder, Pastor, Cathedral of Tomorrow
Akron, Ohio
Mrs. Bobbie James
Alabama's First Lady
Montgomery, Alabama
Rev. Raimundo Jimenez
National Latin American Coordinator
Washington For Jesus
Dr. B. Edgar Johnson
General Secretary
The Church of the Nazarene
Dr. James Kennedy
Pastor, Coral Gables Pres. Church
Coral Gables, Florida
Rev. Charles W. Keysor
Executive Director
Good News Movement

Dr. Dennis F. Kinlaw
President
Asbury College
Violet Kiteley
Pastor, Shiloh Christian Fellowship
Oakland, California
Freda Lindsay
President
Christ for the Nations
Dr. Carl H. Lundquist
President, National Association of
Evangelicals
Rev. Ralph Mahoney
Director
World Missionary Assistance Plan
Dan Malachuk
Publisher
Logos Journal
Dr. Rolf McPherson
President
Int. Foursquare Gospel Church
Dr. John Meares
Pastor, Evangel Temple
Washington, D.C.
Dr. W. Stanley Mooneyham
President
World Vision International
Dr. Lloyd Ogilvie
Pastor, First Presbyterian Church
of Hollywood
Hollywood, California
Rev. John H. Osteen
Pastor, Lakewood Church
Houston, Texas
D. Leland Paris
North and South American Director
Youth With A Mission
Bishop J.O. Patterson
International Headquarters
Church of God in Christ
Sarah Jordan Powell
Singer
Houston, Texas
Rev. John Randall
Pastor, St. Charles Catholic Church
Providence, Rhode Island
Rev. Carl Richardson
Director, Forward In Faith
Church of God
James Robison
Speaker, "James Robison Presents"
Dallas, Texas

Lorne Sanny
President
The Navigators
Father Michael Scanlon
President
College of Steubenville
David Schoch
Pastor, Bethany Chapel
Long Beach, California
Dr. Robert Schuller
Pastor, Community Church
Garden Grove, California
Demos Shakarian
Founder and President
F.G.B.M.F.I.
Rev. Chuck Smith
Pastor, Calvary Chapel
Santa Ana, California
Carlton Spencer
President
Elim Bible Institute
Dr. Charles Stanley
Pastor, First Baptist Church
Atlanta, Georgia
Ken Sumrall
Senior Pastor, Liberty Church
Pensacola, Florida
Dr. Lester Sumrall
President, LESEA, Inc.
South Bend, Indiana
Rev. Chuck Swindoll
Pastor, First Evangelical Free Church
Fullerton, California
Dr. Vinson Synan
Assistant Superintendent
Pentecostal Holiness Church
Dr. Clyde Taylor
Long Time Former President, National
Association of Evangelicals
Iverna Tompkins
Author, Evangelist
Cupertino, California
Rev. Nathaniel Urshan
General Superintendent
United Pentecostal Church
Dr. George Vandeman
Director, Speakers, "It Is Written"
Seventh Day Adventist Church
Bob Walker
Editor-in-Chief
Christian Life Magazine

Dr. C.M. Ward
Long Time Former Speaker,
"Revival Time"
Smallwood Williams
Presiding Bishop
The Bible Way Church
Rev. William Wilson
Pastor, Faith Temple
Rochester, New York
Bishop Jesse Winley
Pastor and General Overseer
Soul Saving Stations
Dr. Thomas Zimmerman
General Superintendent
Assemblies of God

Women's Meeting, Constitution Hall
Monday Afternoon, April 28, 1980

Rev. Anne Gimenez,
program chairman

Shirley Boone

Vonette Bright

Marjorie Horton

Bobbie James

Dee Jepsen

Ann Kiemel

Sarah Jordan Powell

Dede Robertson

Dale Evans Rogers

Nancy Thurmond

Rev. Iverna Tompkins

The Pastors and Leadership Rally
Constitution Hall, Monday evening, April 28, 1980

Pastor John Gimenez,
master of ceremonies

Dr. Bill Bright
David DuPlessis
Ben Haden
William Harness
Dr. James Kennedy
Bishop J.O. Patterson
Dr. Pat Robertson
James Robison
Father Michael Scanlon
Superintendent Nathaniel Urshan
Bishop Smallwood Williams
Bishop Jesse Winley

At RFK Stadium
Monday evening, April 28, 1980

Bart Pierce, master of ceremonies

The Imperials
Bob Birdsong
Nancy Honeytree
Barry McGuire
Truth
Candle
Lamb
Reggie Vincent
Larry Tomczak
Josh McDowell
Crawford Loritts
David Albritton
Keith Green
Noel Paul Stookey
Scott Wesley Brown
Danny Buggs
Pat Boone
The Second Chapter of Acts
Myrna Summers
Nicky Cruz
Arthur Blessit
Larry Andes
Ron Pritchard

Kyle Rote, Jr.
Roger Wiles
The Pat Terry Group

The Rally on the Mall
April 29, 1980

Pastor John Gimenez
Dr. Pat Robertson
Dr. Bill Bright

Dr. Ben Armstrong
Jim Bakker
Tammy Bakker
Rt. Rev. Archimandrite Stephen Barham
Rev. John D. Beckett
Father John Bertolucci
Arthur Blessit
Pat and Shirley Boone
Mrs. Vonette Bright
Rev. Adolfo Carrion
Rev. Morris Cerullo
David Chernoff
John Crossley
Paul Crouch
Gerald Derstine
Dr. Jimmy Draper
Rev. David DuPlessis
John Gilman
Rev. Anne Gimenez
Dr. Charles Green
Ben Haden
Dr. E.V. Hill
Rev. Raimundo Jimenez
Rev. Ben Kinchlow
Dr. Dennis Kinlaw
Rev. Violet Kiteley
Dr. Carl Lundquist
Bailey Marks
Rev. John Meares
Dr. Harold Ockenga

Rev. John H. Osteen
Dr. Leland Paris
Bishop J.O. Patterson
Rev. Garland Pemberton
Father John Randall
Dr. Carl Richardson
James Robison
Dr. Adrian Rogers
Rev. David Schoch
Demos Shakarian
Dr. Carlton Spencer
Dr. Charles Stanley
Dr. Lester Sumrall
Dr. Vinson Synan
Rev. Iverna Tompkins
Rev. William Wilson
Bishop Jesse Winley

*Had time permitted, several
others were scheduled to speak
or sing. Among them:*

The Rev. Steve Brown
Marajen Denman
Don Myers
The Rev. Margaret Oakes
Manuel Roman

Performers:

Fritz Klein as Abraham Lincoln
The PTL Singers and Orchestra
   under Thurlow Spurr
Washington For Jesus Choir (directed by
   Rich Cook and assisted by Hazel Sasser)
Archie Dennis
Evangel Temple Choir
The Rock Church Choir
The Lee College Choir
The Rambos
William Harness

Dannibelle Hall
John Hall
Dana Howard
The Inner City Washington Choir
    with Myrna Summers
Sarah Jordan Powell
Rev. Gilberto Silva
The Hawaiians
Rev. Herbert Bowdoin